D0772532

MANAGING

LONG-TERM

CARE

AUPHA/HAP Editorial Board

Frederick J. Wenzel
University of St. Thomas

G. Ross Baker, Ph.D.
University of Toronto

Sharon B. Buchbinder, R.N., Ph.D.
Towson University

Caryl Carpenter, Ph.D.
Widener University

Leonard Friedman, Ph.D
Oregon State University

William C. McCaughrin, Ph.D.
Trinity University

Thomas McIlwain, Ph.D.
Medical University of South Carolina

Janet E. Porter, Ph.D.
University of North Carolina At Chapel Hill

Lydia Reed
AUPHA

Louis Rubino, Ph.D., FACHE
California State University–Northridge

Dennis G. Shea, Ph.D.
Pennsylvania State University

Dean G. Smith, Ph.D.
University of Michigan

Mary E. Stefl, Ph.D.
Trinity University

Linda E. Swayne, Ph.D.
University of North Carolina–Charlotte

Douglas S. Wakefield, Ph.D.
University of Iowa

MANAGING

LONG-TERM

CARE

Connie Evashwick

James Riedel

AUPHA

HAP

Your board, staff, or clients may also benefit from this book's insight. For more information on quantity discounts, contact the Health Administration Press Marketing Manager at (312) 424-9470.

This publication is intended to provide accurate and authoritative information in regard to the subject matter covered. It is sold, or otherwise provided, with the understanding that the publisher is not engaged in rendering professional services. If professional advice or other expert assistance is required, the services of a competent professional should be sought.

The statements and opinions contained in this book are strictly those of the authors and do not represent the official positions of the American College of Healthcare Executives, the Foundation of the American College of Healthcare Executives, or of the Association of University Programs in Health Administration.

Copyright © 2004 by the Foundation of the American College of Healthcare Executives. Printed in the United States of America. All rights reserved. This book or parts thereof may not be reproduced in any form without written permission of the publisher.

08   07   06   05   04   5   4   3   2   1

Library of Congress Cataloging-in-Publication Data

Evashwick, Connie.
    Managing long-term care / Connie Evashwick and James Riedel.
      p. : cm.
    Includes bibliographical references and index.
    ISBN 1-56793-225-8 (alk. paper)
    1. Long-term care of the sick—United States—Administration. 2. Long-term care facilities—United States—Administration. 3. Aged—Long-term care. I. Riedel, James, CHE. II. Title.
    [DNLM: 1. Long-Term Care—organization & administration. WX 162 E926m 2004]
RA644.6.E976 2004
362.16'0973—dc22

                                         2004047276

The paper used in this publication meets the minimum requirements of American National Standard for Information Sciences—Permanence of Paper for Printed Library Materials, ANSI Z39.48-1984. ∞ ™

Acquisitions manager: Audrey Kaufman; Layout editor: Amanda J. Karvelaitis; Cover design: Megan Avery

Health Administration Press
A division of the Foundation of the
    American College of Healthcare Executives
1 North Franklin Street, Suite 1700
Chicago, IL 60606-4425
(312) 424-2800

Association of University Programs
   in Health Administration
730 11th Street, NW
4th Floor
Washington, DC 20001
(202) 638-1448

To Anita Riedel, my wife and partner of 40 years, for all of her support, encouragement, and love; and to Paul Wozniak, FACHE, deceased, who by example taught me how leaders succeed.

– JR

To Dr. George Evashwick and Dr. Alfred Yankauer, two brilliant, caring physicians, and inspiring mentors.

– CE

Brief Contents

Detailed Contents

Foreword

IT IS AN UNDERSTATEMENT to say that healthcare, including long-term care, is constantly changing. In this changing environment, long-term care managers will be challenged by the increasing expectations of consumers and their families and regulators, tightening resources, and increasing competition. *Managing Long-Term Care* is a much needed introduction to long-term care management and is a first step in preparing prospective long-term care managers and long-term care professionals who are new to management to address these system challenges.

I have viewed the community-based and institutional long-term care system from three perspectives: as a state health policy maker and researcher, as a caregiver and purchaser of long-term care services for a relative, and as a board member of a church-based long-term care system with five continuing care retirement communities and a hospice program. In each of these roles, I have observed the importance of management's role in the organization.

One only has to look at the population trends to see that the first wave of the Baby Boomer generation is approaching retirement. In a few years, the number of potential long-term care users will increase significantly. This generation will be much more economically and functionally independent than earlier population cohorts.

They will want more options for independent living, assisted living, and skilled nursing services, and they will have increased demands and expectations for reasonably priced, quality long-term care services. Regardless of the setting, those individuals who need long-term care services will have more chronic illnesses and will be more dependent in activities of daily living.

Competition has increased among long-term care providers, and many providers are changing their marketing strategies to focus on younger retirees and the amenities that they are seeking within a continuing care retirement community. In addition to demanding more choices and amenities, long-term care service consumers and their families are more litigious, and the number of legal actions against long-term care providers is increasing.

Changes in federal and state healthcare policy, such as the recently enacted Medicare Prescription Drug legislation and the Medicaid funding crisis, impact every long-term care provider. Prospective-payment financing methodologies have been implemented for a number of long-term care providers. The old long-term care business models may not be appropriate for these new payment systems and new customer expectations, placing more emphasis on the importance of strategic planning, excellent managerial skills, and results-oriented performance. Only well-endowed organizations will be able to survive poor financial performance, regardless of the organization's mission and history.

Perhaps no managerial challenge is greater today than maintenance of a well-trained, stable workforce. High staff turnover rates lead to increased operational costs and challenge the manager's ability to maintain quality of care. Enlightened long-term care managers will use Evashwick and Riedel's suggestions in Chapter 4 in recruiting, selecting, and motivating employees to stabilize their workforce.

The long-term care managers of tomorrow must recognize these key environmental changes and adapt their business model to remain competitive. The basic managerial and leadership skills discussed in *Managing Long-Term Care* are the tools managers need to address these challenges and to achieve operational efficiency and effectiveness. The book is well-researched and covers key managerial functions. Part 3, "Managing Your Future," is especially important for a manager's personal development and progression from management to leadership. Evashwick and Riedel used a very thoughtful and well-planned process to involve leading experts in the long-term care field in the development of the book's content and target audience. Examples throughout are very helpful in demonstrating the heterogeneity of the needs of individuals who require long-term care assistance. The examples also illustrate the complexity of the long-term care system, which has multiple funding sources and services, and the necessity of cooperation within the system.

Managing Long-Term Care provides an excellent resource for new long-term care managers, as well as long-term care professionals who are entering a managerial position. Increasing management skills is a key survival strategy for long-term care organizations and is an imperative to achieve improved quality of care and quality of life for long-term care consumers. Successful long-term care organizations will use these improved management skills to adapt to changes in payment, competition, and consumer expectations.

—Thomas E. Brown, Jr., Dr.P.H., M.B.A., CHE
Director, Health Services Research
Palmetto Health
Columbia, South Carolina

Preface

MANAGERS OF LONG-TERM care services and programs face the fundamental management challenges of all administrators. However, long-term care involves a special twist that is different from hospitals, managed care, or other facets of the healthcare delivery system. Clients have serious, long-term problems and may remain with the organization until they die. Caregivers are also important clients, and many are stressed; care may be as much for the caregiver as the client. Financial operations in a long-term care organization may be even more complicated than for acute or ambulatory care, and organizational relationships within the long-term care organization are many and complex.

The purposes of this book are threefold: (1) to introduce students to basic management functions and how they play out in long-term care; (2) to provide those who have come into long-term care with no formal management training a background in management concepts; and (3) to explicate for those already skilled in management concepts how long-term care differs from other healthcare settings. This book does not purport to be a detailed description of management theories, nor a comprehensive delineation of the myriad regulations and laws pertaining to all aspects of healthcare delivery or long-term care. Rather, this book is a structured introduction to management concepts with application to a variety of long-term care settings. The intent is not to provide all of the "answers"—an unrealistic goal for any management text—but to provoke the thinking required for decision making, provide a framework for the issues, and offer sources to pursue for further information.

The first section is an introduction to management, to long-term care services, and to clients of long-term care services. This section offers definitions and an overview of the context of long-term care management. Chapter 1 defines management, offering definitions of the manager's functions and the distinguishing characteristics that make a manager a leader. Chapter 2 introduces the field of long-term care services, its structure, and its financing. Chapter 3 describes the clients: the reason that long-term care services exist.

Part II covers specific management functions, with each chapter devoted to a basic function. Each chapter defines and describes the management function and its key concepts, principles, and select tools. Where appropriate, the book distinguishes how managing long-term care differs from managing other types of healthcare organizations. It also highlights issues a manager is likely to encounter. Each chapter cites examples taken from real-world incidents. These chapters do not attempt to cover every possible situation a manager might encounter, rather, they attempt to identify salient themes and suggest an approach for decision making and action.

Part III focuses on the career of the individual and describes the move from manager to leader, the value of professional association membership, self-assessment of management style, and the importance of life-long learning.

Acknowledgments

WE WOULD LIKE to thank all of those working in long-term care who have shared their insights and experiences with us over the years. We hope this book might be helpful to some of them and to the future cohort of long-term care managers who will follow in their places. May the next generation be as capable!

Our thanks to Mrs. Anita Riedel, who typed and retyped many chapters; Ms. Amanda Garrison, who prepared tables and charts; and Ms. Patricia Fabian, who helped with the finishing touches. Dr. Peggy Smith was an invaluable part of our team as an experienced editor. Four of our peers served as content expert reviewers: Ms. Cynthia Dixon, Dr. Richard Kaffenberger, Mr. Michael Lesnick, and Dr. Louis Rubino—our thanks to them for their time, insights, and honesty in helping to make this a better and more relevant publication. Our thanks to our colleague of many years, Dr. Thomas Brown, who took the time to share his insights in writing the Foreword. As is so often the case, we could not have completed the manuscript without the help of all of these willing and capable colleagues.

We would also like to thank Ms. Audrey Kaufman, the Health Administration Press acquisitions editor who started this project and provided emotional support and functional assistance throughout.

How different was our experience with Health Administration Press, compared to other publishers, because of the personal attention she devotes to each author and book!

Finally, we are grateful to the Archstone Foundation, which provided the funding and the reassurance that this project was worthwhile. Mr. Joseph Prevratil and Ms. Mary Ellen Courtright have made a huge contribution to the field of long-term care, and we would like to acknowledge this on behalf of not only our project but the many long-term care professionals throughout the nation who have received financial and psychological support from the Archstone Foundation's priority for this vital area.

PART I

Introduction

CHAPTER ONE

Leadership and Management

"To live a creative life, we must lose our fear of being wrong.
Leadership and learning are indispensable to each other."

John F. Kennedy (1917–1963)

LEADERSHIP VERSUS MANAGEMENT

Today's long-term care (LTC) services require both strong leadership and superb management. "Leadership" is defined as "to guide someone or something along the way, especially by going in advance; to direct on a course or in a direction" (Webster 1965). Leaders have the ability to take people to places they've never gone before. "Vision," "trail-blazing," "charisma" are words often used to describe leaders. Successful leaders enroll rather than sell people on their vision.

In contrast, "management" is defined as "judicious use of means to accomplish an end" (Webster 1965), and a manager is defined as "one who conducts business affairs with economy and care" (Webster 1965). Managers mobilize people and resources to produce a desired product or service effectively and efficiently. Management deals with the nuts-and-bolts functions of accomplishing daily tasks. Managers may also be leaders, but management activity has a much narrower focus, and management activities have more concrete short-term outcomes, either products or services.

Both strong leaders and effective managers are essential for today's long-term care organization. Resources are scarce, the expectations for the product or service are high, and the environment is constantly changing. Moreover, in long-term care, both functions may be required of the same person. In very large organizations, such as General Motors or Microsoft, hundred of managers populate a company led by a visionary leader whose daily job is to be creative and think "outside of the box." In long-term care the typical organization has many front-line clinical providers, very few managers, and a budget too tight to pay someone just to be the visionary leader. In long-term care, the top manager and organizational leader are likely to be one and the same person.

For these reasons, it's important that all those in management positions understand that their roles may have elements of both functions. It's also imperative that managers in long-term care be skilled at their daily management tasks, thereby generating the self-confidence that underpins leadership. Similarly, knowing the characteristics of leadership may help good managers to break through the specifications of their daily jobs to become leaders. The remainder of this chapter discusses leadership and management in more detail, differentiating the two concepts, but recognizing that in practice, especially in long-term care, they often overlap in an individual.

LEADERSHIP

Leadership is about having a vision of the future and motivating people to achieve that vision. Motivating employees to sign on to the vision is a major concern for all leaders. Although some people are recognized as "natural born leaders," leadership can be learned. Leadership has many styles, and not all work in every circumstance. Leadership may also be situational: people, and the organizations they work in, may need leaders more at some times than others.

Numerous authors and leadership specialists have described the traits of a successful leader. These range from *The Seven Habits of Highly Effective People* noted by Stephen Covey (Covey 1989) to an array of self-help books. Kouzes and Posner capture the essence of

Table 1.1. Ten Commitments of Leadership

Practices		Commitments
Challenging the process	1.	Search out challenging opportunities to change, grow, innovate, and improve.
	2.	Experiment, take risks, and learn from the accompanying mistakes.
Inspiring a shared vision	3.	Envision an uplifting and ennobling future.
	4.	Enlist others in a common vision by appealing to their values, interest, hopes, and dreams.
Enabling others to act	5.	Foster collaboration by promoting cooperative goals and building trust.
	6.	Strengthen people by giving power away, providing choice, developing competence, assigning critical tasks, and offering visible support.
Modeling the way	7.	Set the example by behaving in ways that are consistent with shared values.
	8.	Achieve small wins that promote consistent progress and that build commitment.
Encouraging the heart	9.	Recognize individual contributions to the success of every project.
	10.	Celebrate team accomplishments regularly.

Source: Kouzes, J. M., and B. Z. Posner. 2002. *The Leadership Challenge, 3rd Edition*. San Francisco: Jossey-Bass. Copyright © 2002. This material is used by permission of John Wiley & Sons, Inc.

good leadership in their book *The Leadership Challenge: Five Commitments and Ten Practices of Good Leadership* (Kouzes and Posner 2002). These five commitments and ten practices of leadership are shown in Table 1.1. Anyone interested in improving his or her leadership quotient should consider these suggestions.

To be a leader in long-term care, one must know the field, be sensitive to people, understand the environment, and develop good partnering skills. With this base, the leader must have the organizational authority and the personal self-confidence to create a vision for the future and, if necessary, guide the organization in change (see call-out "Developing Strong Leadership and Effective Management").

MANAGEMENT THEORIES

Whereas charismatic leaders have existed throughout time, management evolved as a science after the Scientific Revolution and, more specifically, during the twentieth century. In long-term care organizations, top staff are often few and the structure shallow; thus, visionary and inspirational leaders at the top must also be skilled managers. They must know the principles, concepts, and standard tools of the basic functions of management.

Over the past one-hundred years, a number of classical management theories have been developed to explain the ways to manage people. A brief summary follows of the major theories and schools of thought that have affected today's managers (Certo 2000).

Scientific Management

Scientific management is attributed to Fredrick Taylor (Taylor 1911). Taylor believed that management of people could be done through scientific application of work methods, productivity, goals, and goal setting. Scientific management purports that "one best way" exists to organize the making of a product.

The focus of scientific management was the production line, and the desired output was a completely standardized physical product. It was a useful theory for mass producing a dependable automobile with parts that could be replaced by any mechanic anywhere in the country. However, the theory was not designed to apply to the service industry, where each client is unique and the "product" is tailored to meet an individual's needs.

Developing Strong Leadership from Effective Management

Diane had joined the Community Nursing Facility as its new director of nurses (DON). She had recently relocated from another state because her husband had been transferred. Although she had complete confidence in her clinical abilities as a nurse, she was still learning the rules that apply to nursing facilities in this new state.

A month later, the administrator unexpectedly resigned. A person from corporate headquarters appeared and announced that she would be the interim administrator. Within two weeks, the interim administrator offered Diane the job of assistant administrator/administrator in training. In six months, she could be the new administrator, with full responsibility for the nursing home.

Diane believed that she was a "natural leader"; she had been president of the PTA at her daughter's school and secretary of her nursing class. She had a good rapport with the staff of the nursing facility, and she believed that the aides and LVNs respected her. She thought being the administrator might give her a chance to bring a new ambiance to the home. On the other hand, she did not know anything about management; her expertise was clinical care. She did not know if six months of on-the-job training would be sufficient to prepare her to take over as both the leader and senior manager of the large home. She could read the licensing exam prep book to find out what she needed to master about management, but she didn't know what being the organization's leader really meant.

Goals, production methods, and timeframes were unilaterally set by management and implemented rather harshly. Employees were viewed as a commodity rather than an asset, differing from modern management theories. The principles of the theory of scientific management are not consistent with today's healthcare management setting, where mutual goals are agreed upon between a manager and an employee, with target dates and completion dates attributed to each goal.

Hierarchy of Needs

A vastly different approach to explaining management comes from Alexander Maslow, whose management theory explains how employees relate to stimuli based on their current level of need (Maslow 1997). Maslow's theory identifies five levels of need, beginning with food and shelter and moving to self-actualization (see Figure 1.1). Maslow's hierarchy of needs posits that if an employee needs shelter, food, and other basic physical essentials of daily living, it is impossible to motivate him with psychological rewards. On the other hand, people who have a home, a car, and a good income are motivated by intangibles, such as commitment, involvement, and having equity in the business, as opposed to receiving a paycheck each week. Maslow remains the most quoted leadership theorist today.

Theory X/Theory Y

Theory X and Theory Y categorizes managers based on their beliefs about employee behavior. Douglas McGregor noted that many managers tend to have attitudes that reflect their belief about workers (McGregor 1960). Simply put, the theory has two sets of manager attitudes. The Theory X manager assumes people dislike work and try to avoid it. Employees must therefore be coerced to perform, since they avoid responsibility and prefer to be directed. In contrast, the Theory Y manager believes people seek responsibility and are creative in solving organizational problems due to commitment. Managers take different approaches to decision making based upon which theory they follow.

Hygiene and Motivation Factors

Fredrick Herzberg put forth the theory that two types of factors are at play in the workplace (Herzberg, Mausner, and Snyderman 1967).

Figure 1.1. Maslow's Hierarchy of Needs

Self-Actualization Needs:
self-fulfillment, achieving full potential

Esteem Needs:
self-image, achievement, competence

Growth Needs

Social Needs:
love, affection, belongingness

Safety and Security Needs:
shelter, employment

Deficiency Needs

Physiological Needs:
food, water, sleep, sex

Source: Maslow, A. 1997. "A Theory of Human Motivation." In *Motivation and Personality, 3rd Edition*, edited by R. D. Frager and J. Fadiman. Copyright © 1997, by permission of Pearson Education, Inc., Upper Saddle River, NJ.

His two-factor theory outlines how hygiene and motivating factors impact employees. Many LTC employers believe that by having good wages, good working conditions, and benefits, employees should be satisfied and motivated. Herzberg sees these as hygiene factors. In other words, they're maintenance factors and keep the employee coming to work but are not motivational. To motivate a person, a job requires other attributes. Hygiene and motivating factors are shown in the accompanying box, "Two-Factor Theory: Hygiene Factors and Motivating Factors."

Systems Theory

Systems theory states that organizations are composed of people, tasks, and structure, all of which are affected by the environment.

Two-Factor Theory: Hygiene Factors and Motivating Factors

Hygiene Factors	*Motivation Factors*
Company policy and administration	Opportunity for
Supervision	achievement
Relationship with supervisor	Opportunity for recognition
Relationship with peers	Work itself
Working conditions	Responsibility
Salary and benefits	Advancement
Relationship with subordinates	Personal growth

Source: Certo, S. C. 2000. *Supervision: Concepts and Skill Building, 3rd Edition*, 212. New York: McGraw-Hill/Irwin. Used with permission.

Organizations are conceived of being like living organisms. Inputs (resources) are transformed by processes into outputs. Outputs are the products of the organization and reflect the organization's goals. Systems theory emphasizes the dynamic flow of organizational activity. Figure 1.2 shows a schematic of the type used to diagram systems management.

LEADERSHIP AND MANAGEMENT STYLES

Personality is an inherent component of leadership and management style. Leadership and management can both be learned, so personality should not really be a factor in prohibiting success. However, behavior may be partially natural and partially learned.

One of the favorite theories used by seminar leaders and others who try to predict management style is the managerial grid theory, first developed by Robert Blake (Blake and Mouton 1964). The underlying premise is that people have tendencies toward a dominant leadership style, and managers of each style interact with employees, co-workers, and superiors in predictable ways. These management styles are called different names by different authors

Figure 1.2. Systems Theory Diagram

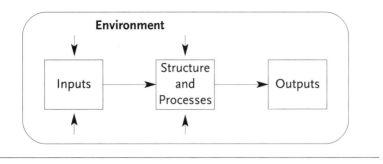

but, in general, fit into four categories: participative, autocratic, task or technical, and laissez-faire.

A variety of tools are available to evaluate management style. The Myers-Briggs instrument is a popular mechanism for self-assessment of personality type, which affects management style. Another tool, the Birkman Assessment, can be used for individual development and executive coaching. This is a set of powerful assessments that reveal human processes and perceptions affecting individuals and their performance in the workplace. Individuals gain insights and tools that lead to personal and professional effectiveness. A "360-degree assessment" is a technique for gaining feedback about a manager's performance from the people with whom he works at all levels of the organization. Each such tool has categories for characterizing style, and most extend these style categories to predict interactive patterns with other professionals, staff, and clients.

Knowing one's own management style, and that of others with whom one interacts, can provide a guide to maximizing effective interaction and avoiding problems. Styles may also vary depending upon the circumstance, and reexamining is useful as career and employment settings change over time.

Long-term care is a people business, whether dealing with clients or staff or referral sources. Thus, styles that facilitate easy interaction with people are particularly useful.

MANAGEMENT COMPETENCIES

Recently, considerable attention has been given to the basic competencies required of managers and leaders in the field of healthcare administration. Ross, Wenzel, and Mitlyng have identified ten areas essential for healthcare administrators to master, regardless of their area of specialization (Ross, Wenzel, and Mitlyng 2002). Thus, the areas apply to those managing long-term care as well as other areas. The ten competency areas are as follows:

1. Governance and organizational structure
2. Human resources
3. Financial management and economics
4. Planning and marketing
5. Information systems
6. Communication and public relations
7. Community health and managerial epidemiology
8. Quantitative analysis and modeling
9. Legal and ethical issues
10. Organizational and healthcare policy

To these might be added the practical considerations of space and physical resource management.

A manager's belief that he or she is knowledgeable about management topics is not enough. Managers must honestly measure their abilities in each competency area to identify opportunities for improvement. Criteria and tools for universal measurement of general healthcare administrators are in the process of being developed (NCHL 2004).

Competency requirements specifically focused on long-term care include those established for licensed nursing home administrators and, increasingly, for those who manage assisted living facilities. The National Advisory Board for Nursing Home Examiners (NAB) has established five competency areas that reflect the areas of information needed to pass the federal nursing home administration examination required by Medicare (www.nab-web.org). Excellent resources for learning the required information and passing the nursing home or assisted living exam have been developed by James Allen (Allen 2003); see www.ltcedu.com for further information.

The purpose of this book is to introduce the reader to the basic management functions that require mastery for ultimate success as a manager of long-term care services. For each topic, numerous books have been written that focus on just that topic, management gurus on these issues speak at national conferences, conceptual frameworks have been articulated, specific tools have been developed, and highly sophisticated software can perform the function on behalf of the organization. This book does not purport to make the reader an expert on all individual management topics, rather, it aspires to provide the reader with basic familiarity, the nomenclature of the topic, core principles, and specific tools.

The specifics of managing long-term care operations will vary with each organization and each state and local context. For specifics about regulations, payment systems, and contracting parameters, the long-term care manager will need to consult local information. Professional and trade associations and state and local governments are typical sources of information, and expert consultants are usually available to assist with specific problems.

Managers are problem solvers and decision makers. No manager, no matter how brilliant, can know everything about all issues. The key to excellence in management is framing the problem based on management fundamentals, knowing how and where to find the information needed to enlighten the problem, and having the confidence to make a decision based on the available information.

SUMMARY

LTC organizations need both leaders and managers. Due to the relatively small size of many LTC organizations, a person must often fulfill both roles. Everyone working in senior management in an LTC organization must be knowledgeable about the basic management functions. In addition, knowing one's style helps tailor performance to the situation. Managers who are confident in their skill and savvy in their relationships with people are then poised to grow into positions of leadership, as well as into top management.

KEYS TO MANAGEMENT SUCCESS

- Differentiate the requirements for a good leader from those for a good manager.
- Learn the basic concepts and tools of the fundamental management functions.
- Assess your own management style. Reassess periodically.
- Be proactive in being positive about people—clients, customers, staff, consultants.

REVIEW QUESTIONS

1. List the differences between leadership and management.
2. Describe five characteristics of effective leaders.
3. Describe four management theories.
4. Explain briefly six fundamental management functions.
5. What is the role of personality and style in leadership and management?
6. What actions can a manager take to assess his or her own performance?

REFERENCES

Allen, J. 2003. *Nursing Home Administration*. New York: Springer Publishing Company. www.ltcedu.com.

Blake, R. R., and J. S. Mouton. 1964. *The Managerial Grid*. Houston, TX: Gulf Publishing.

Certo, S. C. 2000. *Supervision: Concepts and Skill Building, 3rd Edition*, 212. New York: McGraw-Hill/Irwin.

Covey, S. R. 1989. *The Seven Habits of Highly Effective People: Restoring the Character Ethic*. New York: Simon and Schuster.

Herzberg, F., B. Mausner, and B. B. Snyderman. 1967. *The Motivation to Work, 2nd Edition*. New York: John Wiley and Sons.

Kouzes, J. M., and B. Z. Posner. 2002. *The Leadership Challenge, 3rd Edition*. San Francisco: Jossey-Bass.

Maslow, A. 1997. "A Theory of Human Motivation." In *Motivation and Personality, 3rd Edition*, edited by R. Frager and J. Fadiman. Upper Saddle River, NJ: Pearson Education, Inc.

McGregor, D. 1960. *The Human Side of Enterprise*. New York: McGraw-Hill.

National Advisory Board for Nursing Home Examiners. 2004. www.nabweb.org.

National Center for Healthcare Leadership (NCHL). 2004. www.nchl.org.

Ross, A., F. Wenzel, and J. Mitlyng. 2002. *Leadership for the Future: Core Competencies in Healthcare*. Chicago: Health Administration Press.

Taylor, F. 1911. *Shop Management*. New York: Harper and Brothers.

Webster, M. 1965. *Webster's New Collegiate Dictionary*. Springfield, MA: G&C Miriam Co.

CHAPTER TWO

Introduction to Long-Term Care Services

"If we could sell our experiences for what they cost us, we'd be millionares."

Abigail van Buren (1918–)

LONG-TERM CARE (LTC) is the hidden giant of healthcare and social services, involving millions of people every day from a wide array of circumstances and settings. Long-term care services cover a broad spectrum of health, mental health, and related social services. Each service has its distinct operating characteristics. To manage a single service or a set of services, an administrator must know not only that specific service, but also have at least a general appreciation of the management aspects of other LTC services. Given the chronic complex nature of their clients' conditions, LTC services must work together, so a manager must also understand the relationships among services. The purpose of this chapter is to lay out the overall framework of the continuum of long-term care services, highlight the characteristics of the major categories of services, and define the integrating mechanisms in preparation for discussing how to manage these LTC services individually and collectively.

DEFINITION

Long-term care is defined as "a wide range of health and health-related support services provided on an informal or formal basis over an extended period of time to people who have functional disabilities with the goal of maximizing the individual's independence" (Evashwick 2005).

An estimated 80 to 90 percent of long-term care is provided informally by friends and family members (Noelker and Whitlach 2005).

Long-term care services are the formal services used by people with chronic or extended functional disabilities to supplement the informal care provided by family and friends. Some long-term care services may be provided by informal or formal sources, or a combination of the two. For example, a homebound person who needs help bathing may get help one day a week from a family member who comes into the home and another day a week from a formal home care agency. Other services, such as rehabilitation, are available only from formally trained professional providers. LTC services differ from acute care in their goal, which is to maximize functional independence, versus acute care's goal to achieve cure. The categories of formal long-term care services are discussed in more detail in the following section.

SERVICES

LTC services number more than 60 (Evashwick, Rundall, and Goldiamond 1985). For heuristic purposes, these can be grouped into nine categories, based on the setting where the service is most likely (but not always) provided. Table 2.1 shows the broad service categories of the continuum of long-term care. The order of the categories is not fixed. The goal of the long-term care system is to be able to access the configuration of services needed by an individual according to his or her unique needs, and to modify the set of services provided as a person's needs change.

Long-term care services vary in their operating characteristics. Table 2.2 shows key characteristics of select services. This book focuses on generic management functions and how they work in general in long-term care, contrasting LTC with acute care when useful

Table 2.1. Long-Term Care Services

Service Category	Specific Services
Extended Care	Skilled Nursing Facility (SNF) Step-down Unit/Transitional Care Unit Sub-Acute Unit Intermediate Care Facility—Mentally Retarded (ICF–MR)

Acute Care	Hospital Inpatient Units
	   Med/Surg Units
	   Psychiatric Units
	   Geriatric Assessment Units
	   Rehabilitation

Ambulatory Care	Physician's Office Outpatient Clinic Adult Day Care Center
Home Care	Medicare-Certified Home Health Agency Private Home Care Agency Hospice Durable Medical Equipment
Outreach	Information and Referral Meals on Wheels Emergency Response System Telephone Reassurance
Wellness/ Health Promotion	Health Fairs Health Education Programs Disease Management Exercise Programs
Housing	Independent Housing Assisted Living Congregate Living/Group Housing Continuing Care Retirement Community
Functional Support	Transportation Money Management Grocery Shopping Chore Services
Social Support	Congregate Meals Friendly Visitors Telephone Reassurance Senior Centers

Source: Adapted from C. Evashwick. 2005. *The Continuum of Long-Term Care, 3rd Edition.* Albany, NY: Delmar Publishers.

Table 2.2 Sample Operating Characteristics of Select Services

Service	Staffing	Top Payers	Approximate Cost/Unit	Accreditation
Skilled Nursing Facility	1 RN, LVNs, Aides	Medicaid; private	$150/day	JCAHO
Home Care, Medicare	RN, MSW, MD, PT, Pharm D	Medicare; commerical insurance	$95/RN/visit	JCAHO, CHAP
Home Care, Private	On-call staff, professional or support persons	Private pay; commercial insurance; HMOs	$90/hour for RN; $60 for personal assistant	ACHC, NLN, NHC
Hospice	Interdisciplinary team	Medicare; all insurers	$15,000 cap by Medicare	JCAHO, CHAP
Assisted Living	Personal care staff	Private pay	$2,000–5,000/month	JCAHO, CARF
Comprehensive Outpatient Rehabilitation Facility	Rehabilitation therapists	Medicare; commercial insurance; HMOs	Per unit of service	CARF
Meals on Wheels	Volunteers	Older Americans Act	$2/day fee	None

JCAHO—Joint Commission on Accreditation of Healthcare Organizations
CARF—Commission on Accreditation of Rehabilitation Facilities
CHAP—Community Health Accreditation of Rehabilitation Facilities
NLN—National League of Nursing
NHC—National Homecaring Council
ACHC—Accreditation Commission for Home Care

to do so. However, each long-term care service has its own operating profile. These differences pose a challenge to a manager who is trying to integrate care from the perspective of the client across services and over time. Long-term care is also highly local in its organization and heavily influenced by state regulation and financing. Thus, every local long-term care system will have its own unique composition and characteristics. One of the tasks of the long-term care administrator is to be able to overcome differences across services to facilitate integration. The more an administrator knows about management functions in general and about specific long-term care services, the easier it is for the administrator to create valid ways to achieve coordination of care for the client's benefit.

INTEGRATION

In brief, long-term care is a highly fragmented array of services, with different operating characteristics and different payers, that the administrator must try to make seamless from the standpoint of the client who should ideally receive comprehensive, continuous, appropriate clinical care without disruption. The vignette "Encountering Long-Term Care Services" illustrates how many services a single episode of illness may involve and how complex it is to orchestrate all the services required by a single individual.

Long-term care services are intertwined in their use because of the nature of long-term care. Clients tend to use multiple services, either simultaneously or sequentially. A long-term condition that inhibits a person's physical functioning over a long period of time may affect their mental well-being (depression may set in), economic situation (funds spent, no income as a result of inability to work), social situation (loneliness and isolation), and housing (unable to remain in his or her own home). Thus, a broad spectrum of services may be needed over time. Moreover, even the initial medical services a person requires may change and thereby cause a change in the configuration of support services needed.

Encountering Long-Term Care Services

Mrs. Jones is a 78-year-old woman who lives alone in a three-story brownstone walk-up in the middle of a large city. One February, she slips on the ice and breaks her hip. She is taken to the emergency room and then transferred to surgery for a hip replacement. She then begins a long process of long-term care. Over a six-month period, she goes from the hospital to the skilled nursing facility to a rehabilitation hospital to home care with meals on wheels and a friendly visitor, then to adult day services. She also receives case management, counseling by a social worker for depression, durable medical equipment, and, finally, outpatient rehabilitation therapy. After six months, she is once again walking and living independently, but she has experienced a wide array of services (and has lots of bills to prove it!).

Four Integrating Mechanisms

Figure 2.1 shows the conceptual continuum of care with the major service categories and the cross-cutting integrating mechanisms. Four fundamental integrating mechanisms are used to coordinate care across services and over time (Evashwick 2005):

1. Inter-entity management coordination
2. Clinical coordination/case management
3. Integrated information systems
4. Integrated financing

Inter-entity management coordination refers to the structures and processes that enable organizations to coordinate all facets of client care, from clinical to administrative. These include a wide range of management techniques, from formal transfer agreements to automatic dial on the phone system. Organizations strive to put in place management structures that enable independent professionals, staff, clients, and families to achieve continuity of care as a client receives services from more than one provider or payer.

Figure 2.1. Integrating Mechanisms for the Continuum of Care

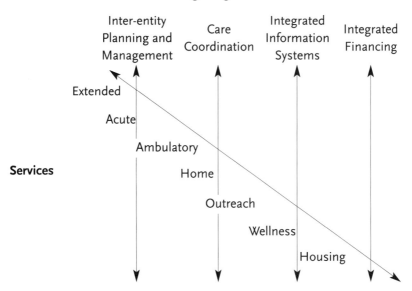

Integrating Mechanisms

Inter-entity Planning and Management · Care Coordination · Integrated Information Systems · Integrated Financing

Services

Extended · Acute · Ambulatory · Home · Outreach · Wellness · Housing

Source: Adapted from C. Evashwick and L. Weiss. 1987. *Managing the Continuum of Care*. Gaithersburg, MD: Aspen Publishers.

Clinical coordination refers to coordinating the clinical services that are rendered to a person by a variety of different providers over time. Unless deliberate effort is made by the clinicians, information is frequently not transferred. Case management has become a common way to coordinate care. Other mechanisms include interdisciplinary teams and primary care physicians.

Integrated information systems refers to sharing data from multiple data sources. Within an organization this means combining clinical, management, and utilization data. These types of information can be shared across organizations as well, as comprehensive data sets or as more limited sub-sets of data. The technology exists to create an entirely automated, comprehensive information set for each client. The federal government is prompting private parties to move in this direction. However, numerous barriers have prevented a comprehensive, fully-integrated information system from being the norm. In sharing information, privacy, security, and confidentiality must be respected, as required by the Health Insurance Portability and Accountability Act (HIPAA).

Integrated financing refers to pooling financial resources from multiple payment systems. This provides flexibility to clients and removes barriers caused by eligibility criteria, service limits, and insurance coverage. However, the regulations accompanying most types of healthcare financing, particularly government programs, currently restrict the prevalence of integrated finance. New models are being tried at state levels that bode well for financial integration for LTC services in the future.

A more detailed description of the services and integrating mechanisms is available in Evashwick's *The Continuum of Long-Term Care* (2005). The challenges facing managers of long-term care include implementing each of these integrating management mechanisms across services for the ultimate goal of seamless client care.

POLICIES AND IMPACT ON SERVICES

Long-term care services are affected by federal, state, and local policies. Despite an array of legislation at all levels, the United States has no single policy for long-term care and, thus, no articulated comprehensive system for providing or paying for long-term care. The result is that each service is affected by multiple laws and regulations, and any two long-term care services may be governed by totally different laws. For example, laws governing mental health services are totally distinct from legislation governing Veterans Affairs health services. However, a single individual with a mental condition may receive services at both a mental health center and a Veterans Affairs medical center. It falls to the administrator of the service to establish the policies and procedures by which clinical staff coordinate across the two systems and by which agency payment is sought and allocated appropriately.

The accompanying box shows select major laws affecting long-term care services. Legislation typically covers one or more of four categories of programs: resources (such as buildings or manpower), financing (Medicaid, Medicare), direct service (Veterans Affairs Health System), or regulations (Balanced Budget Act of 1997). Managers of LTC services face a very challenging task in developing the management functions that coordinate complex sub-systems of care created by different legislation at different points in time.

Major Federal Legislation Pertaining to Long-Term Care

Social Security Act, 1935
Veterans Administration, 1963, 1972, 1975, 1980
Mental Health Acts, 1963, 1967, 1971, 1986
Title XVIII (Medicare), Social Security Act, 1965
Title XIX (Medicaid), Social Security Act, 1965
Older Americans Act, 1965; latest reauthorization, 2001
Housing and Urban Development Act, 1965, 1974
Developmental Disabilities Services and Facilities Act, 1970
Title XVI (Supplemental Security Income), Social Security Act, 1972
Rehabilitation Act, 1973
Title XX, Social Security Act, 1974
Omnibus Budget Reconciliation Act, 1987
Medicare Catastrophic Coverage Act, 1988
    (repealed 1990)
Americans with Disabilities Act, 1990
Patient Self-Determination Act, 1991
Family Medical Leave Act, 1993
Health Insurance Portability and Accountability Act, 1996
Balanced Budget Act, 1997
National Caregiver Support Act, 2000
Ryan White Care Act, 1990, reauthorized 2000
Medicare Prescription Drug, Improvement, and Modernization Act,
    2003

Source: Evashwick, C. 2005. *The Continuum of Long-Term Care, 3rd Edition*. Albany, NY: Delmar Publishers.

At a local level, the entities regulating LTC are as fragmented as the services themselves. Identifying the details of state regulations that govern a service may require accessing multiple agencies. The best source of information about state and local requirements may be colleagues running similar services and/or state professional or trade associations.

Lobbying for long-term care is another aspect of a manager's job that becomes very important in a field with so many competing advocacy groups and such frail clients. Professional and trade associations can be effective in mobilizing a constituency to advocate effectively for changes to improve the system. An administrator of a long-term care service may feel that day-to-day operational tasks are so overwhelming and essential to the care of individuals that there is no time for participation in the political process. However, to attain the changes needed to improve the fragmented, underfunded approach that currently exists, involvement by skilled and knowledgeable long-term care leaders is essential.

IDEAL SYSTEM

Most professionals working in long-term care share a philosophy about what the service delivery system should offer clients. An ideal system as a goal provides a standard by which to evaluate the current system and identify the gaps between the existing and the ideal. Ideally, a comprehensive continuum of care would do the following (Evashwick 2005):

- Match resources to the client's condition, avoiding duplication of services and use of inappropriate services
- Take a multidisciplinary approach to the client's and family's situation
- Monitor the client's condition and modify services as needs change
- Coordinate the care of many professionals and disciplines

- Integrate care provided across a range of settings
- Streamline client flow and facilitate easy access to services needed
- Maintain a comprehensive record incorporating clinical, financial, and utilization data across settings
- Pool or negotiate to achieve comprehensive financing

Managers working with today's LTC organizations strive to achieve these characteristics for each individual service, as well as to bridge the fragmentation that exists to be able to offer comprehensive, coordinated care across settings. LTC managers, especially those in leadership positions, have the long-range goal of creating permanent changes in LTC system structure and financing.

SUMMARY

The continuum of long-term care is more than a collection of fragmented services, it is an integrated system of care composed of both services and integrating mechanisms. The framework presented consists of eight major service categories and four essential integrating mechanisms. To coordinate client care effectively, a manager must know the basic operating characteristics of all the services frequently used by the LTC organization's clients. The organization must consciously implement the four integrating mechanisms to coordinate service delivery. LTC managers must actively work for change for the future by participating in advocacy efforts and the policy process.

KEYS TO MANAGEMENT SUCCESS

- Know the basic operating characteristics of each service.
- Consider ways to coordinate care better within the LTC organization.

- Explore ways to coordinate care better with other health and social service organizations.
- Be involved in the policy and regulatory development processes.

REVIEW QUESTIONS

1. Define long-term care.
2. What features distinguish long-term care from acute care?
3. How many formal long-term care services have been identified? List 10.
4. On what operational characteristics do long-term care services vary? Give examples.
5. Why does a manager need to know about the operating characteristics of more than just the service he or she manages?
6. Name three categories of public policy that affect long-term care.
7. What are the four integrating mechanisms and how does each contribute to the coordination of care?

REFERENCES

Evashwick, C. 2005. *The Continuum of Long-Term Care, 3rd Edition.* Albany, NY: Delmar Publishers.

Evashwick, C., T. Rundall, and B. Goldiamond. 1985. "Hospital Services for Older Adults: Results of a National Survey." *The Gerontologist* 25 (6): 631–37.

Noelker, L., and C. Whitlach. 2005. "Informal Caregivers." In *The Continuum of Long-Term Care, 3rd Edition*, edited by C. Evashwick. Albany, NY: Delmar Publishers.

CHAPTER THREE

Clients, Including Families

"Every one of us is given the gift of life, and what a strange gift it is. If it is preserved jealously and selfishly, it impoverishes and saddens. But if it is spent for others, it enriches and beautifies."

Ignazio Silone (1900–1978)

BY DEFINITION, PEOPLE who need long-term care are unable to care for themselves. They may be physically able, but mentally need help. Conversely, they may be mentally completely competent, but physically disabled. The conditions and the needs of long-term care recipients vary widely.

Families are the customers for long-term care services every bit as much as the clients themselves. They are the caregivers, the advocates, and often the bill payers. Families can make the job of the LTC administrator and staff easier or more difficult.

Managers of LTC services must know both their clients and the clients' families to provide direct care. They must know their market well to attract the clients and families they wish to serve. The purpose of this chapter is to characterize the clients and families who use LTC.

RATIONALE

Clients of long-term care become involved with their care providers on a personal basis in a way that is not possible during the short stay of acute care. The clients of long-term care establish relationships with the providers of services that are far more personal and intense than the relationship of clients in more acute services. Several reasons underlie this. First, those receiving long-term care interact with the caregivers over an extended period of time. The opportunity exists for people to get to know each other as individuals.

Second, long-term care involves multiple aspects of a person's being, including the person's family relationships, financial status, educational background, and activity preferences. Planning and implementing an effective care plan may require decisions made on the many facets of a person's situation, not just clinical status. Finally, personality and behavior are often involved in long-term care in a way not applicable to acute care. Motivating a client and fostering a change in attitude may be as important as clinical care itself in achieving goals and maximizing function.

LTC is about people helping people. The human dimension permeates all aspects of long-term care. Managers must thus be adept at dealing with clients, families, and staff. The latter are dealt with in the next chapter. This chapter deals with clients and families.

CARE RECIPIENTS

Millions of people receive long-term care each year. Table 3.1 shows the number of people receiving just select types of LTC services.

In keeping with the definition of long-term care as services broadly provided to someone who is unable to function independently without assistance, the recipients of long-term care span a wide spectrum in their characteristics: economic and demographic status, health status, mental status, housing, social support, financial status, underlying diagnosis, type of care received, duration of care, and beginning and ending functional status. Clinical diagnosis alone is not sufficient to make someone a user of formal long-term care

Table 3.1. Users of Select Long-Term Care Services, 2002

Service	Number of Clients
Nursing home	2.5 million/year
Adult day service	85,000/day
Medicare home care	2.7 million/year
Medicaid home care	5.1 million/year
Hospice care	885,000/year

services. Eighty to ninety percent of long-term care is provided by friends and family members. For every person who receives care in a nursing home, two equally ill people are cared for at home. Thus, use of formal long-term services reflects a person's social support as much as health status. Table 3.2 shows the prevalence of various conditions that might result in use of formal or informal long-term care services.

The common characteristic of those who need long-term care is the inability to function independently. The activities of daily living (ADLs) and instrumental activities of daily living (IADLs) are two measures of functional ability. The ADLs are a well-defined set of physical activities involving gross motor functions. Dr. Sidney Katz and colleagues first defined the ADLs through a research study (Katz et al. 1963). References to ADLs have come into common and pervasive use. The ability to perform the ADLs is usually lost by an individual sequentially, that is, the first basic function a person gives up doing themselves is typically bathing; the last function a person is unable to do without help is eating.

Instrumental activities of daily living, or IADLs, refer to daily activities that require fine motor skills and/or cognitive reasoning. The list of activities is less structured than that for ADLs. Examples are shown in the box "Activities of Daily Living (ADLs) and Instrumental Activities of Daily Living (IADLs)."

ADLs and IADLs are evaluated by systematic ratings of the degree of independence. Although many scales have been developed,

Table 3.2. Selected Chronic Health Conditions that Limit Activity Among Adults, 1998–2000

Chronic Health Condition	Number of Affected Adults per 1,000 Population, by Age			
	18–44 years	45–64 years	65–74 years	75 years and over
Mental illness	10.4	18.6	11.4	10.7
Diabetes	2.6	18.5	38.4	42.5
Fractures/joint injury	6.8	15.9	25.4	48.6
Vision/hearing	4.2	13.8	31.2	82.5
Heart/other circulatory*	5.4	45.5	110.8	170.9
Arthritis/other musculoskeletal	22.0	73.2	117.8	193.1

* Includes complications from a heart problem, stroke, problems with hypertension or high blood pressure, and other circulatory system conditions.

Source: Pastor, P. N., D. M. Makuc, C. Reuben, and H. Xia. 2002. "Chartbook on Trends in the Health of Americans." In *Health, United States*, Figure 17, p. 64. Hyattsville, MD: National Center for Health Statistics.

most evaluate the person's ability with a scale that differentiates able to perform with no assistance, requires assistance from a device, requires assistance from a person, or not able to perform.

DEFINITIONS

In defining its target market, an LTC organization should use definitions consistent with those used by the healthcare field. Several that are key to LTC are below.

Chronic is defined by the National Health Interview Survey as a condition that lasts 90 days or more (Adams and Marano 1995). Chronic conditions may be permanent, or a person may recover, but after an extended period of time.

Activities of Daily Living (ADLs) and Instrumental Activities of Daily Living (IADLs)	
ADLs	*IADLs*
Bathing	Cooking
Dressing/grooming	Shopping
Ambulating	Money management
Toileting	Telephoning
Transferring	Housekeeping
Continence control	Chores
Eating	Doing laundry
	Using transportation

Impairment is a permanent physical or mental condition that may (or may not) inhibit a person's performance of ADLs or IADLs (Adams and Marano 1995).

Disability refers to the inability to perform independently one or more of the ADLs or IADLs, regardless of the underlying cause (Adams and Marano 1995).

Client Terminology

The clients of long-term care are referred to by various terms, and use of appropriate terminology is important (see Table 3.3). Nursing facilities and assisted living facilities refer to *residents*. Homecare agencies use *clients*. Durable medical equipment suppliers, having more of a retail orientation, may use the term *customers*. People attending adult day health are referred to as *participants*. Only those providers who derive from the medical model, such as hospitals or rehabilitation, use the term *patient*. Throughout this book, the term *client* is used as the most generic referent.

Terminology is part of the ambiance of the LTC organization and one means of showing respect for the individuals who are

Table 3.3. Terminology for Senior Clients, by Service

Service	Terminology
Skilled nursing facilities	Residents
Assisted living facilities	Residents
Adult day care centers	Participants
Home health agencies	Clients
Durable medical equipment suppliers	Customers
Senior centers	Seniors
Hospitals	Patients
Physicians	Patients

receiving care. One task of the managers is to ensure that those to whom the organization is providing service are called by the appropriate name. This can be accomplished by including terminology as part of staff orientation, having managers always use the correct term, and making sure all written materials have correct wording. Employees heard to use improper terminology should be reminded of the preferred wording even if no clients are present. Particularly new staff or staff who have switched from one long-term care setting to another, or contract staff who switch from setting to setting, may need help with this. A number of other terms are used for special sub-populations.

Children with special health care needs (CSHCN) refers to children who do not meet baseline criteria for mental or physical functioning appropriate for their age. According to federal laws, CSHCN are eligible for special services provided through the education, health, and social welfare systems. Some may outgrow the problem and no longer meet the criteria. Others may turn 18, thereby aging out of the category and accompanying service benefits, and become an adult with a disability.

Persons with disabilities is the current terminology to refer to people who have (primarily) physical disabilities that limit the person's ability to function independently. The change from an earlier referent as *the disabled* reflects the positive approach of stressing what a person is able to do rather than what he or she is not able to do.

Developmental disabilities (DD) are mental conditions that affect a person's physical functioning and independence in activities that require cognitive processing. People with such disorders should not be referred to as *the developmentally disabled,* but rather as people who have developmental disabilities. With new medications, those with DD and similar behavioral conditions may be mainstreamed and not even recognized as members of a distinct group by the general population.

People who are *mentally retarded* are people whose IQ falls below a specific standard. These people are more appropriately referred to by long-term care providers according to the services they are receiving rather than their diagnostic condition. For example, *residents* of a group home, *participants* of a day care program, or *clients* of a case management agency.

Throughout this book, the term client is used to refer to the people who receive any type of long-term care service.

Age Disparities

Providers should also have a policy about how to refer to individuals receiving care. In many instances, care providers are young, and those they care for are older. Providers should be clear with clients about their name preferences. If a care recipient prefers to be called by first or last name, this should be noted. Staff should not automatically call care recipients by their first name. Terms of endearment, such as "deary" or "honey," as well as clearly or potentially disrespectful terms, should be avoided unless the care recipient and care providers develop familiarity and rapport. Care providers should be clear with staff, care recipients, and families about the organization's name policies.

CULTURAL AND LANGUAGE ISSUES

The primary language and native culture of care recipients affect a person's preference for care and how they react to it. For example, some religions and cultures have specific foods that are not acceptable. Any LTC organization that provides meals must be sensitive to these customs to gain acceptance by their clients.

Language can pose a barrier to communication, particularly between staff and recipients of care. Many locations in the United States have high immigrant populations speaking a primary language other than English. Recent immigrants are a significant component of the LTC workforce, since they are often willing to work for the entry-level wages typically paid to support staff of many LTC organizations. For example, in Los Angeles, a large Orthodox Jewish population of former Russian immigrants has now aged in place, and caregivers are often Spanish-speaking recent immigrants from Mexico and Latin America.

The inability to communicate and understand cultural preferences may have a negative impact on care or recruitment of new clients. The LTC organization must be aware of potential differences and act to reduce potential problems. The workforce should be trained in cultural sensitivity, provider practices should be examined with an eye toward cultural preferences and language barriers, and methods should be in place to handle cultural or language problems that may occur.

Positive outreach to a particular culture or language group can be a marketing technique that will attract new clients to the LTC provider whose competition may be unwilling to accommodate. For example, a facility in California added signage in Khmer and hired a Cambodian social worker as a response to the large Cambodian community. An Area Agency on Aging in Massachusetts contracted with a local senior center to establish a monthly meal program for Indian clients, who otherwise were not inclined to participate in senior center activities.

PATIENTS' RIGHTS

Respect for the individual is a fundamental tenet of the nation, and is also required by Medicare of its providers. As one of the conditions of participation, each agency or facility that contracts with Medicare and Medicaid must make public the patients' bill of rights that it implements on behalf of clients. Accreditation agencies tend to follow Medicare's lead in requiring providers to pay attention to the needs of their clients beyond immediate care and to notify clients of their rights. Written statements of a patients' bill of rights or referral to where they can be obtained are posted for easy client access. More than just as a compliance measure for regulations, a patients' rights policy is useful to clients, families, and staff alike to set the tone for care and communication. LTC managers should use these documents as tools to educate staff about appropriate interaction with clients and families.

FAMILIES

Families are the customers of long-term care services every bit as much as the care recipients. Families are the caregivers, the advocates, and often the legally and financially responsible parties. Families can make the administrator's job easy or complicated, rewarding or discouraging. Recent nationwide surveys indicate that about one-fourth of all families, or about 52 million adults, are caregivers (Noelker and Whitlach 2005).

For example, it is not uncommon for residents of nursing facilities to experience loss of personal property. Loss of something small, like a ring, may be blamed on staff, even if the claim is false. The administrator may know nothing about the incident until they receive an angry call from the resident's family. Problems like this can be minimized with policies in place, staff training, and a practice of open communication between staff, administration, families, and residents.

Managers who deal with families to create a mutually positive experience follow the basic principles of involvement, communication, and respect for the opinion of others. In general, LTC organizations should approach families as participants in their family member's care and determine how each individual family member wants to be involved. Methods for dealing positively with families include the following:

- Establish communications channels, and make them known.
- Keep family informed about the services provided, as well as the care for the individual family member.
- Provide opportunities for family involvement in the organization, such as picnics, parties, lunches, etc.
- Establish guidelines for family participation in care, such as grooming, visiting, bringing food, etc.
- Promote staff and family communication (e.g., make sure staff know how to introduce themselves and explain what care they are providing).
- Encourage families to educate themselves about their loved ones' conditions through tapes, videos, books, and websites.
- Establish conflict resolution mechanisms—let families know how to express their complaints, and whom to call.
- Have policies in place regarding responsibilities for clients' personal belongings. Bridge the line of wanting care recipients to feel comfortable by having their possessions surround them, versus the risks of loss or damage.
- Help families with caregiving stress, demands, and boundaries.

Client-Family Dynamics

Not all relationships between care recipients and families are positive, and formal providers may get caught in the middle of dysfunctional interpersonal dynamics within a family. For example, one sibling may want to pay for a private room for the mother, and another may want to pay only for a shared room but a private aide. Similarly, family caregivers and clients may not always agree. For example, a social worker or case manager may order a service to benefit the client that the client rejects. It is the manager's job to enable staff to do the job for which they are responsible, to protect the organization from wrongdoing and lawsuits, as well as to respect the client and provide them with compassionate care.

SUMMARY

People needing formal LTC services have a wide variety of physical and mental conditions, as well as cultural and language differences. They have in common the inability to perform independently the activities of daily living (ADLs) or instrumental activities of daily living (IADLs). Families and friends provide the vast majority of care. The formal LTC service delivery system complements the informal system. LTC organizations must accommodate the families as well as the direct care recipients. Management practices and processes should be developed with sensitivity to the client and family and should promote family involvement whenever possible.

KEYS TO MANAGEMENT SUCCESS

- Remember that LTC is about people. The primary reason for being in business is to provide care to people unable to care for themselves.
- Create an atmosphere of respect for all individuals.
- Establish communication vehicles and channels.
- Encourage expression of opinion and preferences by the individual, including clients, staff, and family members.

- Accommodate individual preferences, including language and cultural preferences, as much as possible without jeopardizing organizational performance.
- Know your clients and their families individually.
- Monitor and strategize how to meet the needs of your aggregate target customer base.

REVIEW QUESTIONS

1. What are ADLs? IADLs?
2. Give examples of the range of physical and mental conditions that may cause a person to become functionally disabled.
3. What factors determine whether a person will need formal long-term care or be cared for informally?
4. What are management actions that an LTC organization can take to succeed with families of LTC clients?
5. Give examples of the terms for clients used by different LTC services.

REFERENCES

Adams, P. F., and M. A. Marano. 1995. "Current Estimates from the National Health Interview Survey, 1994." Vital Health Stat 10 (193). *National Health Interview Survey*, Appendix II, p. 137. Washington, DC: U.S. DHHS, National Center for Health Statistics.

Katz , S., A. Ford, R. Moskowitz, B. Jackson, and M. Jaffe. 1963. "Studies of Illness in the Aged." *Journal of the American Medical Association* 185: 914–19.

Noelker, L., and C. Whitlach. 2005. "Informal Caregivers." In *The Continuum of Long-Term Care, 3rd Edition*, edited by C. Evashwick. Albany, NY: Delmar Publishers.

PART II

Management Functions

CHAPTER FOUR

Human Resources

""The true measure of a man is how he treats someone
who can do him absolutely no good."

Samuel Johnson (1709–1784)

Ms. Cathcart, administrator of Community Care, brought her management staff together to discuss the problem of staff turnover. Community Care is a multi-level LTC complex, with assisted living, a private home care agency, and an adult day center. During the past year, the staff has turned over 100 percent. Some positions have been vacant twice. The owner, Mr. Louis, is perplexed. He thought he had hired good people at the top, and they were supposed to hire good people for all the other positions. Since the organization is new, Mr. Louis had empowered the senior managers to create all the job descriptions so that they could establish duties as they wanted. He wasn't sure they had gotten around to doing this before they, too, quit. Ms. Cathcart was hired as the latest administrator and charged with her number one priority of stopping the turnover.

Prior to the meeting, John Watts, director of facilities and maintenance, reviewed the problem as he saw it and jotted down notes in preparation for the meeting. His assessment centered around two major items. First, there was the problem of salaries not being consistent with the outside market. Mr. Watts estimated the agency was about 20 percent behind the general market. The second problem he saw was the lack of visibility of the administrator and her lack of communications with staff employees.

At the management meeting Ms. Cathcart began by outlining the problem as she saw it. She concluded that the problem centered in three areas: (1) poor selection procedures by management staff and the need for additional management training in selection procedures; (2) the need for closer supervision of employees by management; and (3) the need to improve organizational commitment by providing better employee activities, such as annual picnics.

John Watts was about to challenge Ms. Cathcart's conclusions when several of the other managers voiced their agreement with the administrator's conclusion.

THIS CHAPTER SUMMARIZES basic human resource functions. First, an understanding of the importance of people to the organization and an overview of the long-term care workforce provide a context for human resource activities. Human resource functions are then examined, and the criteria for a human resources plan presented.

THE VALUE OF PEOPLE

Employees are a major key to running an efficient operation and a critical factor in gaining competitive advantage. Many successful companies attribute their success to the attitude and industry of their employees. Staff are critical in achieving all management functions. Successful executives realize that without the staff, little gets accomplished. However, time and resources must be invested in staff by the organization to warrant their loyalty, energy, and creativity.

Most LTC services depend on a very small management staff and a large clinical or direct care staff. Without dependable front-line staff and competent department managers, the business will not survive. As the leader relies on employees to make decisions further down the line, it is essential to develop staff competencies that enable employees to take on increasingly responsible roles in management of the organization, as well as their clinical care. In LTC, front-line workers with little formal training often make independent decisions in settings where clinicians and managers may not be present. For this reason, staff competencies become all the more important.

LTC organizations often have a staff representing widely varying competencies: highly trained clinicians who may work on a part-time consultation basis with highly focused client interaction, and front-line caregivers with little education who work full-time with challenging clients. Establishing policies and processes to empower these two widely varying types of staff is particularly challenging for the LTC organization. In brief, an LTC organization cannot take human resources for granted; adequate time, thought, and resources must be committed to the full spectrum of human resource (HR) functions.

THE LONG-TERM CARE WORKFORCE

The challenge of HR in LTC organizations revolves around the characteristics of the workforce. As indicated above, the workforce for long-term care consists of large numbers of personal care assistants with minimum formal training and a much smaller number of highly skilled professionals, primarily therapists and nurses. Highly skilled clinicians command high salaries, while the personal care assistants with less education and lower skills may be working at or near minimum wage. As an example, Table 4.1 depicts major occupational categories involved in home health care, along with corresponding median hourly rates.

Other types of LTC organizations display comparable differences between the lesser skilled occupations and the more highly paid clinicians. A survey of wages conducted by the Center for the Health Professions found that of 26 health professions, nursing aides, orderlies, attendants, and home health aides were the lowest wage categories (Center for the Health Professions 1999). Salaries for physical therapists were three times as high as those for personal care assistant–level

Table 4.1. Average Compensation of Home Health Agency Caregivers, October 2001

	Average Hourly Rate
Occupational Therapist	$23.84
Physical Therapist	$20.82
Registered Nurse	$20.59
Speech/Language Pathologist	$18.84
Medical Social Worker	$15.84
Licensed Practical Nurse	$14.66
Respiratory Therapist	$14.42
Home Care Aide III	$ 8.12

Source: National Association for Home Care/HCS. 2001. *Homecare Salary & Benefits Report, 2000–2001*. Washington, DC: NAHC/HCS.

staff. These low wages make it difficult to keep morale high when staff confront the difficult work of caring for people with functional disabilities. In addition, low wages and few, if any, benefits make it hard for LTC organizations to compete with other entry-level positions in other fields, such as fast food operations, that have easier tasks.

For those who do want to be in the health field, LTC organizations must compete with other healthcare organizations, which offer higher wages and benefits. For example, in 2002, the median annual salaries for nurses were $49,190 in hospitals; $45,890 in home health care services; and $43,850 in nursing care facilities (Bureau of Labor Statistics 2004).

Personal care assistant positions are projected by the Bureau of Labor Statistics to be among the most highly demanded positions in the future. This prediction forebodes even greater competition for LTC organizations.

Difficult job content, low wages, poor or non-existent benefit packages, and competition from other industries create high turnover among the unskilled occupational categories of LTC employees. High turnover rates mean the LTC organization is constantly recruiting. Among the unskilled workforce, this high turnover also means training demands on the organization that must recognize low levels of education and literacy.

High turnover and many new staff affect quality, as well as costs, of the LTC organization. LTC organizations must seek to meet quality standards while continuously losing and adding staff. New recruits may be willing, but face a learning curve in both knowledge and skill.

At the opposite end of the skill dimension, professional clinicians such as therapists and nurses are in short supply and high demand, and thus command higher wage and benefit packages. Given the high competition, the LTC organization must create attractive options to recruit and retain the professional segment of the workforce.

HUMAN RESOURCE FUNCTIONS

Human resource (HR) functions include the following activities:

- Recruiting
- Selecting employees
- Designing salary and benefits
- Appraising performance
- Motivating employees
- Training employees
- Managing labor relations
- Complying with legal and equal opportunity regulations

Large organizations, such as healthcare systems or multi-facility corporations, are likely to have an entire department devoted to these functions, as well as a director of HR whose sole responsibility is managing HR activities. In small LTC organizations, these functions may all become the responsibility of one person or may be divided among a team of senior managers. The following sections describe each of the HR functions.

Recruiting

As noted above, LTC organizations face fierce competition for staff because of the nature of the work. At the level of "unskilled" workers, such as aides and personal care assistants, LTC organizations compete with numerous employers that also pay close to minimum wage. Many, such as fast food companies, pay about the same as LTC providers but offer much easier working conditions. The difficulty of LTC tasks, such as toileting heavy residents and changing bedpans, hardly compares to shaking fries at a fast food restaurant or making change in a department store. However, as later sections note, the relationship with clients may provide non-monetary rewards.

At the skilled level, LTC organizations compete with hospitals and ambulatory care providers for nurses, therapists, counselors, and other highly trained personnel who tend to be in short supply and command high wages. Volunteers assist in many social service–oriented LTC entities, but this source of labor is undependable and competes with other organizations for volunteers' personal preferences.

Due to high market competition and high turnover, LTC organizations tend to be constantly recruiting. Most LTC organizations tend to recruit from the outside, especially when recruiting for clinical or technical positions. However, considering career ladders both within a single discipline and across disciplines and providing cross-functional training opportunities can help LTC providers recruit and retain a strong and committed staff.

For external recruitment on an ongoing basis, the organization should produce a generic advertisement that can be supplemented with specific job descriptions when needed. Paid advertising can display ads on a regular basis; job description flyers can be posted at little cost among the community network of long-term care providers; and outreach activities provide the opportunity to recruit. Internet methods for recruiting include tapping into HR-specific sites, circulating emails, and participating on listservs that reach the target audience. Close working relationships with high schools and junior colleges help build a steady flow of labor, especially when the LTC organization can work with the educational institution to have students trained with essential skills before they take a job. Accepting local university student trainees also contributes to productive recruiting. Successful LTC organizations that have high turnover try to build a reputation of "always looking for good people."

Personnel who choose long-term care and remain in the field tend to do so because of a personal love of the field and the clients. Advertising for employees or contractors, whether verbal or in writing, should stress these personal benefits.

Selecting Employees

Several tools can improve the LTC organization's success in selecting the right employees and matching employee skills to organizational needs. Typically, the well-managed organization will use job descriptions, objective evaluations, and interviewing to aid the selection process.

Job Descriptions

Job descriptions are the cornerstone of human resources. The job description helps in recruiting, selecting, training, conducting performance appraisals, setting compensation, and abiding by the law. Well-written job descriptions facilitate the staff selection process. The job description defines the minimum qualifications and experience needed and becomes a screening tool. Minimum requirements set the floor for hiring specifications and for starting salary. The job description outlines the tasks, duties, and responsibilities of a job. It is also the basis for the performance appraisal, raises, promotions, and even terminations, if they become necessary. Job descriptions can be written in many ways. The accompanying example shows elements of information that are often included.

Many LTC organizations do not develop proper job descriptions with sufficient detail. Gathering information so that a detailed job

Sample Job Description

Staff Psychologist
Reports to: Director of Professional Services
Department: Professional Services   Division: Resident Care
Date: Approved:

Job Summary:
Under the direction of the Director of Professional Services, this position is responsible for providing family, individual, and group therapy; psychological testing and evaluation of residents; monitoring treatment-planning efforts; participating as a member of the clinical team; contributing to staff education.

Essential Functions:
The person in this position is responsible for:
1. Family, individual, and group therapy when indicated.
2. Psychological testing and evaluations of residents.
3. Participation, facilitation, and documentation of the treatment-review team process, in concert with the Director of Professional Services.
4. Monitoring treatment-planning efforts on residential units, shelter, and community-based programs, in concert with the Director of Professional Services.
5. Acting as a treatment and resource person for line staff in the residential, shelter, and community-based programs.
6. Attending residential, shelter, and community-based programs.
7. Monitoring case records to ensure quality and professionalism, in concert with the Director of Professional Services.
8. Attending court hearings at the request of the Director of Professional Services.
9. Acting as a resource person to the educational department.
10. Submitting feedback of observations to the Director of Professional Services on a weekly basis.
11. Ongoing needs assessment for staff-training purposes, and assisting in the implementation of in-service training programs in cooperation with the Director of Professional Services.
12. Developing and aiding in the implementation of new treatment

programs under the supervision of the Program Director and Director of Professional Services.

13. Supervising any interns working on the treatment units.
14. Collaborating as a team member with other clinical specialists, including physicians, contract professionals, and staff employees.

Additional Responsibility:
Represent the organization at community meetings upon request by the Program Director or Director of Professional Services.

Knowledge, Skills, and Abilities:
1. Highly developed ability in the administration, scoring, and interpretation of psychological tests, specifically objective, projective, and neurological test batteries.
2. Highly developed verbal and written communication skills in English. Proficient in producing reports, according to established computerized protocols.
3. Demonstrated skill in clinical interviewing.
4. Demonstrated ability in group therapy, group management, individual therapy, and family counseling.
5. Supervisory skills to oversee the work of interns and staff assigned to the psychology lab.
6. Demonstrated skills in consultation, and the ability to work as part of a team.
7. Knowledge of billing procedures and approved billing codes.

Education and Experience:
1. Minimum of a master's degree in psychology from an accredited educational institution.
2. Experience in the human services field.
3. State license.
4. Provider billing license.

Other:
1. Must demonstrate good attendance.
2. Must be on time, especially for clinical appointments with residents and families.

description can be written might use interviews, questionnaires, and observation. Other tools might include employee records, industry standards, external regulations, or information from professional trade associations or other similar groups. Once approved, job descriptions must be kept current.

Assessing Candidates

Ideally, the candidate selection procedures identify employees whose job success can be predicted. Most organizations have applicants submit a formal application but also seek information about candidates from external sources such as references, background investigations, and medical exams. Many LTC organizations have evolved from community-based agencies, and hiring has not always been a rigorous process. The absence of a rigorous hiring process can create performance problems and may cost the organization money, clients, quality ratings, and resources.

Because of the small size and flat organizational structure of many LTC organizations, the administrator and senior managers are often subject to pressures to hire based on personal connections. These pressures can be avoided or minimized if a formal application procedure is in place and linked to well-written job descriptions. Thus, formalizing the job application process helps protect the management and the organization from hiring the wrong person for the wrong reason.

Interviewing

Interviews are extremely useful in evaluating candidates. This is especially true for LTC organizations where most positions are highly people oriented. Interviewers should be well-versed about the specific job description and work requirements. Interviewers should also receive training in proper interviewing techniques and equal opportunity laws and procedures. The interviewing process should use the same set of questions for each candidate and have an objective rating scale for each question. This enables the interviewer to look back after interviewing several candidates and to compare candidates.

Moreover, a qualitative approach minimizes or eliminates unfounded discrimination. Recruiting employees is an expensive process, and making good choices helps the organization's financial status as well as employee morale.

Designing Salary and Benefits

The organization's approach to salaries and employee benefits will affect the organization's ability to attract and maintain employees and consultants. Salaries in LTC are typically low, and, benefit packages are often meager or non-existent, compared to other healthcare organizations. These factors make it challenging for LTC organizations to compete for staff with hospitals, health plans, and other healthcare employers. Fortunately, salary and benefits are not considered the only motivational factors. Giving employees a sense of belonging and recognition of a job well done are also powerful motivators. However, salary and benefits must be consistent with those of the outside market to attract and retain qualified personnel. The design of the salary and benefits program need to meet the criteria in the callout box "Criteria for Effective Compensation Plans" to be competitive.

As indicated above, many LTC organizations do not provide employee benefits, except those that are mandated by law. However, many LTC organizations have been creative in developing other benefits that attract employees. For example, an intergenerational program for clients of an assisted living complex might combine a day care center for children of employees with recreation and nurturing opportunities for residents. Such programs have strong appeal and direct economic implications for workers. Scholarships for attending university classes are worth more than direct salary because they are not taxed as income. Assuming salary and benefits are consistent with the local market, building a culture of caring is the single greatest magnet for those organizations that wish to attract and retain good staff.

Criteria for Effective Compensation Plans

Benefits Plans
1. Employee input into design
2. Cafeteria style with basic coverage and employee choice beyond
3. Meets market standard
4. Meets budget/cost criteria
5. Well-communicated to all employees and managers

Wage and Salary Plans
1. Based on worth of the job internally
2. Salary ranges based on an actual review of the marketplace
3. Consistently applied policies that are communicated well to employees and managers
4. No secrets about program ranges or how the salary program is administered
5. Merit increases based on performance criteria

Appraising Performance

Performance appraisals are useful tools to motivate employees to higher performance levels as well as to address potential problems. LTC organizations range from highly regulated to not regulated at all, and some are forced by external regulations to develop employee performance programs that satisfy compliance, licensing, quality assurance, or accreditation demands. The majority, however, will be able to define their own performance appraisal system.

An effective appraisal system is typically based on job descriptions, which should be current. The appraisal should address the following questions:

- What are the standards of performance?
- Do employees know these standards?
- What measures are used to assess these standards?
- How often is performance measured?

- Has management been trained to conduct performance appraisals?
- Is there a self-evaluation process that employees can use?
- How are results communicated to the employee?
- How do the appraisals relate to rewards, monetary and other?
- Are there opportunities to recognize outstanding performance by the employee beyond the job description and the formal appraisal?

Performance appraisals, if properly implemented, can serve to improve employee work habits and employee commitment while meeting organization goals. Successful appraisal systems include invited participation, requested self-assessment, and appreciation expressed for work done. The person conducting the appraisal should meet with the staff member in person to review the evaluation. The discussion should minimize criticism and focus on problem-solving. The session should be supportive, establish goals, and provide for regular follow-up. Properly implemented performance appraisals can improve communications and provide direction to employees.

For LTC organizations that use contract professionals or that use a registry to supplement staff at all levels, evaluating personnel performance with the same process may not be possible. Nonetheless, a process must be developed to evaluate registry and contract staff according to the same values used for permanent staff. Performance expectations should be built into the contracts with organizations or individuals. In addition, professionals may have their work evaluated as part of the quality assurance process. Otherwise, the LTC organization's expectations should be built into the original or renewed contract as specific criteria for the arrangement. Such criteria might include not only quality of care, but performance methods, such as completing all records on time.

Implementing Progressive Discipline

Occasionally LTC organizations employ staff that are simply not suited for long-term care. When this occurs, management's duty is to help counsel the employee to find another area of work outside long-term care. In such cases, counseling to move to another line of work is in the best interest of the institution and the staff member.

Employees who have disciplinary problems need to be dealt with in a different way. Many organizations have adopted a progressive discipline program to handle such situations. This program gives the management and the employee the opportunity to correct undesirable behavior, but it also provides a way for management to deal effectively with the problem employee in a progressive manner.

Typical employee disciplinary problems include:

- Lack of cooperation or interest
- Poor productivity
- Tardiness or absenteeism
- Dress code violation
- Disregard for safety issues
- Insubordination
- Time card violation

When such offenses occur, an organization with a progressive discipline program has a staged approach by which to deal with the problem. Actions at all stages should be recorded in the employee's record.

The earliest stage is verbal counseling. Verbal counseling would be given as the first step in a progressive discipline program for minor violations.

The second step in such a program is written reprimands or warnings. Written reprimands are given for repeated minor infractions or for the first-time occurrence of a more serious offense.

The next step is usually a final written warning or suspension. In such situations, the employee receives a final written warning indicating that he or she will be terminated if the inappropriate behavior is not corrected. In the case of a suspension, an employee will usually be suspended without pay for several days in an attempt to get the employee's attention regarding a major offense or the continuation of repeated minor offenses.

Termination is the final phase in progressive discipline. An employee may be terminated for repeated minor violations (e.g., repeated absenteeism) or serious violations (e.g., safety risks), or for a major offense of a critical nature (e.g., unacceptable practices in caring for a client).

Most sophisticated LTC organizations should consider having a progressive discipline program in place in an effort to try to get employees back on the right track and preserve their employment. Retention is the preferred outcome for both the employee and the LTC organization.

Some LTC organizations use a 90-day probationary period to assess how well an employee is predicted to perform. A probationary period might be used for new employees, and the progressive discipline program for those with longer service. If both methods are used, it is important that they be written and applied as distinct measures, and the meanings communicated to employees at the outset of employment and discipline.

Motivating Employees

Staff need to embrace the vision of the organization and develop a sense of equity to feel motivated and contribute enthusiastically. Motivating staff takes a multi-faceted approach. Salary and benefits tend to be primarily maintenance items, and LTC organizations need to find additional motivations to promote commitment of employees. One way to increase employee commitment is to increase their sense of involvement. This can be done at no or low cost—it is an attitude of information sharing and an approach of delegating authority based on trust.

Given the low operating budget of many LTC organizations, methods of motivation have to be creative: offering day care, creating an on-site employee bank to make small loans, inviting staff children to attend LTC organization parties, or giving loans or scholarships for formal education. Consistently communicating with staff, involving staff in the organization's vision and goal attainment, building trust through responding to staff questions—these are all factors that motivate. In addition, consistent and good supervision is a top motivating factor in modern organizations.

Training Employees

Every LTC organization should develop a systems approach to training and development. The systems approach examines what the organization needs, what resources are available internally to conduct training, and what must be performed by external resources. The systems approach also considers training required by law, both orientation and continuing education, and how the success of training will be measured. In addition, the LTC organization should consider what skills it will need for the future and encourage or require staff to attain the essential skills so that the organization's existing staff stays current.

Training in LTC organizations requires a combination of orientation and on-the-job training. The management must ensure that each new employee has completed appropriate orientation and training prior to assuming job responsibilities. LTC organizations also must develop solid methods for management development. Different types of management training include on-the-job experiences, seminars and conferences, and management retreats that include education.

A combined approach to training is usually used. Training may be done in-house by using existing staff or by bringing in a consultant. Alternatively, staff can be sent out for training sessions of various lengths put on by the government, trade or professional organizations, universities, or community organizations. The budget for education should recognize the different levels of training needed; the amounts; the different formats; and the associated costs.

The LTC organization needs to rely on management staff to develop the employees. Managers need to develop their employees' abilities to acquire superior knowledge and skills, through continuous training, to enhance their work performance. Solid management practices should include developing training programs that complement the skills employees bring to the job and enhance their ability to perform work tasks, as well as enhance their own individual careers. Cross-training and using managers and senior clinical staff to conduct educational in-services are ways to promote education without incurring significant additional expenses. Staff within the LTC organization are likely to have a wealth of expertise that can be shared; they need a conducive venue and format to do so.

In addition, within LTC, developing career ladders for people who wish to stay in the field is important. Many organizations have found that developing ladders of opportunity allows employees to gain more responsibility and earn more money, while reducing turnover within the organization. Collaborating with local universities, offering scholarships, and articulating job changes linked to education or skill improvement are all ways to promote job ladders without excessive expense.

Managing Labor Relations

Labor relations has many complex legal and technical components. Seeking assistance from professional labor relation consultants is recommended. A brief summary of the select issues is provided here.

The topic of labor relations frequently evokes concerns regarding unionization. Proper communication and relations with employees will help avert unionization. Several key issues, all within management's control, have been leading reasons for employee unrest in healthcare organizations and lead employees to seek union representation. The issues that contribute to such unrest include reduction in staffing levels, poor supervision, lack of job security, poor communications, and lack of management involvement. Addressing these issues proactively can help LTC organizations avoid employee dissatisfaction.

While executives must keep salaries as competitive as possible, they also must communicate to staff their sincere efforts in this regard. Everyone would prefer higher salaries. However, when staff believe that client care is suffering as a result of budget cutbacks, they react. When managers reduce staff without showing staff how to rearrange work tasks to compensate for those reductions, the burden is placed on staff to balance reduced manpower levels with the same workload. Frustration also increases if staff have no input in staffing levels or in rearranging work.

Employees have the legal right to organize or refrain from joining a union. A complex set of laws and regulations governs the union organizing process. In 1974, the Taft-Hartley Act (Labor-Management Relations Act) was amended to include coverage of employees working in private hospitals and nursing homes. These amendments establish requirements governing the collective bargaining process related to the patient care issues in such facilities. Additional information is available on the right to organize and union organizing campaigns from various labor relations sources, including seminars, books, professional organizations, and the Internet.

In brief, the manager of an LTC organization who wishes to foster good employee relations and remain union-free should consider the following questions:

1. Are staff communicated with frequently and truthfully?
2. Are staff allowed to ask questions or bring up any issue at meetings? Are questions answered responsively?
3. Are financial issues and reimbursement challenges shared with staff?
4. Are salaries and benefits competitive with the outside labor market? Are compensation policies well-understood by staff?

5. When staff reductions are necessary, are staff assisted in learning new work patterns or multi-skilled so patient care is unaffected?
6. Do staff have input into staffing issues?
7. If layoffs are necessary are they handled by length of service? Is length of service valued in employee relations?
8. Does the organization recognize and reward employee contributions to patient care or to the organization?

Executives understand the challenges of keeping their organization vibrant as well as financially solvent. Sharing these challenges honestly with staff and engaging them in finding solutions helps employees feel involved. When employees understand the problems of the organization, they tend to become involved in solutions.

COMPLYING WITH REGULATIONS

A variety of federal and state laws govern any organization's hiring practices and continued employment of employees. Although a few laws apply specifically to LTC organizations (e.g., training of nurses' aides for skilled nursing facilities), the majority apply to employers of all types. This topic is far too broad to cover comprehensively here. The following is a brief overview of the most common areas of concern:

• The Equal Pay Act of 1963 requires employees covered by the Fair Labor Standards Act and state compensation laws to receive equal pay for equal work regardless of sex. This pertains particularly to employees engaged in interstate commerce and government employees.
• Title VII of the Civil Rights Act of 1964, amended in 1972, 1991, and 1994, prohibits discrimination in employment on the basis of race, color, religion, sex, and national origin. It

also created the Equal Employment Opportunity Commission (EEOC), which enforces the provisions.

- The Age Discrimination Act, enacted in 1967 and amended in 1986 and 1990, prohibits discrimination for persons over the age of 40.
- The Pregnancy Discrimination Act of 1978 broadened the definition of sex discrimination to include pregnancy, childbirth, and related medical conditions and prohibits termination due to pregnancy. It also prohibits treating childbirth as a medical condition.
- The Americans with Disabilities Act, passed in 1990, prohibits discrimination against people who are disabled in terms of access and right to employment.

Table 4.2 presents a more detailed listing of federal laws pertaining to equal opportunity employment. In addition, each state may have pertinent laws.

The LTC organization must have policies that ensure compliance with all these laws. Professional and trade organizations and external consultants are valuable resources. In addition to including this information in policy documents, senior managers should periodically review these policies to ensure that they are current with legal requirements and that the organization is implementing practices consistent with the law.

These principles also apply to vendors and consultants as well as employees. For example, the worker's compensation allocations should be established within the accounting system that produces payroll. The accountant, who in small LTC organizations is usually a consultant rather than employee, must know the appropriate amounts required by the state to withhold, and accounting software should be programmed to do this automatically. When the law changes, both the accountant and the software vendor should update the accounts of the LTC organization. However, since the onus falls on the organization to make sure it is current, periodic reevaluation of compliance is necessary. The LTC organization should specify in its contracts with vendors and consultants that changes to the law will be incorporated into their work and the LTC organization notified.

THE HUMAN RESOURCES PLAN

HR initiatives should be consistent with the organization's strategic and business plans, as well as accommodate changes in the external environment. Ideally, effective organizations should have a well-articulated plan that guides their HR efforts.

In an LTC organization that is part of a large vertically integrated healthcare delivery system or a horizontally integrated multi-facility long-term care system, a formal human resources plan may be done internally or by external consultants and updated periodically. In a small LTC organization, the various components of the HR plan may be the responsibility of the administrator or delegated to another senior manager. In such situations, the components of the plan are condensed and much information is gathered from secondary sources, such as professional or trade associations. In reality, most small LTC organizations seldom have a well-articulated HR plan. Nevertheless, knowing the essential elements considered important to a formal HR plan can raise awareness of important HR considerations.

A formal human resources plan should have at least eight elements, as described below:

1. *Analysis of the local labor market.* The manpower plan contains an annual analysis of the workforce marketplace. This analysis will identify the most difficult jobs to recruit and current market rates for salaries and benefits. Wage and workforce information can usually be determined from a trade or professional organization, many of which conduct annual workforce analyses and report salary schedules on behalf of their members.

Table 4.2. Federal Equal Employment Opportunity Laws

Source	Purpose	Coverage	Administration
Fifth Amendment, U.S. Constitution	Protects against federal violation of "due process"	All individuals	Federal courts
Thirteenth Amendment, U.S. Constitution	Abolishes slavery	All individuals	Federal courts
Fourteenth Amendment, U.S. Constitution	Provides equal protection for all citizens, and requires due process in state action	State actions (decisions or government organizations)	Federal courts
Civil Rights Acts of 1866 and 1871	Establishes the rights of all citizens to make and enforce contracts	All individuals	Federal courts
Equal Pay Act of 1963	Requires that men and women who perform equal jobs receive equal pay	Employers engaged in interstate commerce	EEOC* and federal courts
Civil Rights Act of 1964 (+Title VII), amended in 1991	Prohibits discrimination on the basis of race, color, religion, sex, or national origin	Employers with 15 or more employees who work 20 or more weeks per year, labor unions, and employment agencies	EEOC

Law	Description	Applies to	Agency
Age Discrimination in Employment Act of 1967	Prohibits discrimination in employment against individuals 40 years of age and older	Employers with 15 or more employees who work 20 or more weeks per year, labor unions, and employment agencies	EEOC
Rehabilitation Act of 1973	Protects individuals with disabilities against discrimination in the public sector and requires affirmative action in the employment of individuals with disabilities	Government agencies and federal contractors and subcontractors with contracts greater than $2,500	OFCCP**
Americans with Disabilities Act of 1990	Prohibits discrimination against individuals with disabilities	Employers with more than 15 employees	EEOC
Executive Orders 11246 and 11375	Prohibits discrimination by contractors and subcontractors of federal agencies and requires affirmative action in hiring women and minorities	Federal contractors and subcontractors with contracts greater than $10,000	OFCCP
Family and Medical Leave Act	Requires employers to provide 12 weeks of unpaid leave for family and medical emergencies	Employers with more than 50 employees	Department of Labor

*EEOC: Equal Employment Opportunity Commission; **OFCCP: Office of Federal Contract Compliance Programs

Source: Fried, B. J., and J. A. Johnson (editors). 2002. *Human Resources in Healthcare*, Table 4.1, p. 64–65. Chicago: Health Administration Press.

2. ***Identification of key jobs.*** Each organization needs to identify the key jobs that represent the majority of its employees. These jobs are easily recognized and typically common to other similar organizations; hence it is relatively easy to collect relevant market information on job characteristics, such as licensing requirements and salaries. The results of a compensation and benefits surveys for key jobs will be useful in wage and benefit negotiations. Comparative information is usually available through a trade association.

3. ***Analysis of turnover.*** Conduct exit interviews or survey employees who have left. Long-term care is an extremely demanding field, especially for direct care providers. Salaries are low for those who provide caregiving support services, and the emotional and physical demands are high. The entire field experiences considerable turnover, but some organizations experience even more turnover than their competitors. Unusually high turnover, either in the entire organization or in a single department, usually points to a management problem. Quality of care and client satisfaction are directly related to staff morale. Hence, it behooves the LTC organization to identify why staff leave and to correct identified problems.

4. ***Evaluation of retention rates and reasons.*** Why people stay with an organization is more important than why they leave. If an organization knows why its employees are satisfied, these factors can be modeled in other departments. Consulting with staff to determine what is "right" in their department will help in designing other programs. Individual meetings with key leaders, meetings with department heads, or group meetings with staff are all ways to solicit staff input.

5. ***Forecast of demand.*** A look into the future will reveal what new skills will be required. Assessing demand for skills based on the changing nature of the workplace will help forecast the need for employees who can fill specific job niches in the future. External forces may also affect demand. For example, new licensing or continuing education requirements promulgated by

state government or new types of paraprofessionals authorized by Medicare will change who the LTC organization must hire and at what price.

6. *Forecast of surplus or reduction of staff.* When an imbalance in skills occurs, it is troubling for managers to be involved in layoffs while simultaneously hiring employees with other skills. If turnover can be forecast, layoffs can be avoided or minimized by combining natural turnover with a strong retraining program. The executive management team (see Chapter 5) working together may be able to transfer staff across functional lines within the organization if work imbalances can be predicted.

7. *Maintenance of competitive salary and benefits.* Employees are the most valued asset of most LTC organizations. Maintaining a strong competitive salary and benefits program goes a long way to reducing turnover and retaining staff. To do so, the LTC organization must keep abreast of the market and maintain a position that is equal to or greater than the market in both salary and benefits for the types of jobs that it recruits.

Understanding that long-term care reimbursement is generally less than optimal, the LTC organization should nonetheless adopt a policy to pay attention to the total compensation level provided to employees. If salary and benefits are viewed as an easy way to save money or balance the budget, employees will move on to better paying organizations or consider unionizing. Rather than saving money by cutting positions, the LTC organization should review work processes and change the way the staff works to be more effective and efficient. Using reengineering and multi-skilling methods will help reduce costs and still provide good care and compensation.

8. *Achieve strong labor relations.* Remaining union-free is an important consideration for all LTC organizations. Employees generally join unions when wages and salary are so far out of line with the market that it becomes an important issue. Employees also have a tendency to look for union

representation when they perceive a lack of job security or poor management and supervision in the organization.

If employees organize, it will be more difficult for long-term care management to deal with employees, and costs will increase. Long-term care managers should maintain competitive salaries, provide reasonable benefits, assure themselves that those in supervisory positions are communicating with staff, and allow staff to have input into their work situation. Conduct periodic communication meetings with staff, allowing staff to ask questions without regard for their job security. A fair compensation package and an honest communication program are keys to achieving a strong labor relations program within the organization and avoiding loss of control to a union.

SUMMARY

People are the heart of long-term care. A comprehensive human resources program must be maintained by all LTC organizations, regardless of size. The specific functions include recruiting, hiring, establishing wages and benefits, conducting performance appraisals, dealing with unionization threats, and engaging employees in ongoing education. The LTC organization must comply with the myriad of federal and state laws pertaining to equal opportunity and human resource functions. Despite the physical and emotional challenges of working in long-term care, the field does have appeal. Human resources must emphasize the positive aspects of the job and the human benefits that exceed standard wage/benefit considerations.

KEYS TO MANAGEMENT SUCCESS

• Develop a well-organized HR function that clearly articulates how each of the basic HR functions is accomplished.

- Reinforce the value of job descriptions in all HR endeavors including selection, performance appraisal, promotion, and legal issues. Keep job descriptions current.
- Ensure that compensation and benefits truly reflect the competitive labor market and communicate efforts to employees.
- Use the performance appraisal process to further engage staff.
- Develop employee incentives in addition to salary and benefits.
- Adhere to EEO and other labor regulations.
- Establish a manpower planning program to anticipate human capital needs and react to changes in the labor market.
- Establish a culture of ongoing education for staff at all levels.

REVIEW QUESTIONS

1. What characteristics of the LTC workforce pose challenges to those responsible for human resources?
2. What are the primary human resource functions?
3. What strategies can aid LTC organizations in recruiting and retaining staff?
4. Identify major legislation that governs hiring and employment practices.
5. What elements should a formal HR plan include?

REFERENCES

Bureau of Labor Statistics. 2004. www.bls.gov/oco/ocos083.htm, April 5.

Center for the Health Professions. 1999. *The Hidden Health Care Workforce.* San Francisco: University of California.

CHAPTER FIVE

Management Teams

"Credit is like peanut butter: spread it around...
you will be surprised how far it goes!"

John Alexander has been the administrator of Homecrest Home Health Agency for the past year. John has come from the for-profit industry and managed many LTC facilities as the director of finance. During his first week on the job, he calls his management team together to discuss how he will communicate with them.

He has decided the most time-efficient and effective way to involve each individual is to meet with them one-on-one rather than on a group basis. As a result, he plans to schedule weekly meetings with each member. At those meetings they discuss what needs to be done in their area of responsibility and how it is to be carried out. John believes this will be the most effective approach, because it saves his time, leaving him more time for his objectives, and it will reduce the arguing that always seemed to occur at group meetings at his last place of employment.

After reviewing current financial statements, John is in the process of requesting budget reductions in all areas. He has just met with each individual manager and requested a 5 percent budget reduction. John is surprised at the reaction from the managers. Disharmony reigns; each manager wants to know what the others have to cut. Most feel they run efficient departments, and there is no need for reduction. In fact, the feeling among most managers is that they have already cut more than others. Everyone except for the CFO feels that there is no need for reductions.

THIS CHAPTER OUTLINES the steps to bring together an effective management team able to move the LTC organization into the future. One of the challenges in most LTC organizations is the sparse number of managers. It becomes incumbent on the administrator, therefore, to develop an executive management team that is cross-functional as well as effective. If properly constituted and allowed to work as a true team, management teams can become so effective that the organization succeeds far beyond the group's expectations.

DEFINITION

A team is a group of individuals who work together to solve problems and manage one or more organizational activities. *Teamwork* is defined as "work done by several associates each doing a part but all subordinating personal prominence to the efficiency of the whole" (*Merriam-Webster's Collegiate Dictionary* 2003). The element of surrendering individual identity for the benefit of joint activity is critical.

A team is different from a committee. Ideally, teams involve the same people over an extended period of time, whereas committee members may change on a periodic basis. The work of a team is ongoing, whereas committees may have discrete or time-limiting tasks. Committee members are often appointed specifically to represent their perspective, in contrast to teams, where individual disciplines or departments or other identity is merged into overall team identity.

From a semantic point of view, a team may be formally called a *committee*, but actually function as a team. Committees are seldom referred to as *teams*.

Types of Teams

Teams can be formed for a number of purposes, such as clinical teams (e.g., rehabilitation), or specific management functions (e.g., quality assurance). The focus of this chapter is the executive management team, which assumes responsibilities that represent the major management responsibilities for the organization. In a large multi-faceted organization, the management staff may be large in number, and a team approach used only selectively. In a small LTC organization, with only a few managers and perhaps only one senior administrator with a very broad span of control, the executive management team approach can be extremely beneficial. It is a concept of the senior managers working together to solve problems and run the LTC organization smoothly.

BENEFITS AND DRAWBACKS

Management teams can bring great strength to an organization. This is not done, however, without training, time, and trust—so the benefits to the organization and the individuals must outweigh the costs.

Benefits

Management teams have been used effectively in industrial and healthcare organizations for many years. Because of the small number of managers, most LTC organizations have a hierarchical organization, with the CEO taking on many functions that tend to pull decisions to the top level. The management team approach is superior to the hierarchical one for several reasons. The benefits to an organization include the following:

- Joint problem solving
- Back-up available
- Shared workload
- Better communication
- More collective history
- Increased manager cross-training

- Reduced feeling of isolation
- Enhanced organizational loyalty
- More fun!

By pooling their knowledge and using group synergy to spark creativity, effective management teams are able to solve organizational problems quickly and better than an individual could. Those responsible for support functions, such as billing and hiring, learn to appreciate the tasks of the front-line staff, especially client care, and vice versa, creating a more supportive environment for all staff.

The characteristics of many LTC organizations make a team approach to management particularly valuable. Many LTC organizations have relatively few senior managers, and the administrator often has a very broad span of authority. If an executive management team can be developed, responsibilities can be shared and spread across several people. This expands the knowledge base used to make decisions, the conveyors of information, and the leaders available to mentor junior staff. In addition, should the administrator be absent or not available, others are empowered with the knowledge and the authority to make a decision and enable the organization to solve problems.

Drawbacks

Building team rapport takes time, both intense time that the team spends together, and months, if not years, of working together. Individuals must abandon their egos, their discipline-specific biases, and their functional role in favor of organizational well-being. Building trust and learning to function as a team requires effort from all members. Some of the factors that make building management teams difficult are listed below:

- Time available during the workday for team meetings is limited.

- Education and effort are required beyond performing one's regular job.
- Cross-training may be required.
- Turnover impedes progress.
- Egos may get bruised.
- Lack of self-confidence of LTC managers inhibits participation.
- Personalities may not be amenable.

All of these barriers can be overcome if an organization is committed to developing a team. The senior administrator or CEO needs to commit to sharing power, authority, and knowledge with the team, as well as to making available the resources that will be needed to cultivate and empower individual team members.

SIZE AND COMPOSITION

The size and composition of a team vary with each organization and each type of team. The total staff size of the organization, the geographic disbursement, the number of management staff, the scope of services, and, most of all, the purpose of the team are all factors that affect how many people will be on the team. Ultimately, the senior administrator determines the initial size and composition; later the team itself may decide to add others.

An executive management team in a typical LTC organization usually ranges from three to ten members. If much larger, the team is likely to become unwieldy and lose the cohesion important for teamwork.

The executive management team should include those who are responsible for major business management functions, such as finance and marketing, and select clinical functions, such as nursing and social work. However, the team should not simply look like a list of department heads, as some departments perform support activities and others perform core business activities. Moreover, because of the shallow structure of many LTC organizations, managers are likely to have responsibility for a broad range of functions that might encompass several departments in a larger healthcare organization. Figure 5.1 shows an organization chart for a typical long-term care organization and identifies potential members of the executive management team. Key functional areas that should be represented on the management team include:

- Finance
- Human relations
- Key clinical services
- External relations and contracts

TEAM DEVELOPMENT

Katzenbach and Smith (1993) describe the challenge of building an effective team as follows:

> People on real teams must trust and depend on one another—not totally or forever—but certainly with respect to the team's purpose, performance goals, and approach. For most of us, such trust and interdependence do not come easily; it must be earned and demonstrated repeatedly if it is to change behavior.

Simply convening a team of individuals does not ensure cohesion. A group cannot be brought together and expect immediate transformation into a team exhibiting solidarity. For teams to work effectively, they must work together for a considerable length of time. Bringing cross-functional teams together for individual problem solving where the team might work on a problem for two to four meetings is generally a step in the right direction, but this alone is not sufficient.

For an effective team, members must work together for long periods of time and must recognize the perspectives of other members.

Figure 5.1. Organizational Structure in Long-Term Care

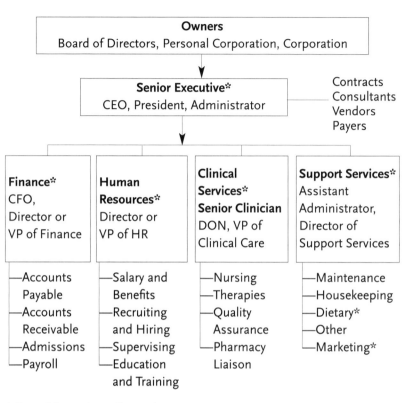

* Potential members of executive management team

Whereas client care staff in LTC organizations tend to exhibit high turnover, managers are much more likely to stay for an extended period of time. The time required to build team unity is critical, and, to a certain extent, team development must start over every time a new person is added.

A team must develop sensitivity toward how members participate. Since the team members will be working collaboratively to solve problems, plan, and make decisions, the members need to communicate effectively. The team's initial foray into group decision making may well be uncomfortable, since the management team members will not be accustomed to suggesting solutions in areas outside their individual areas of responsibility. A facilitator can often assist in identifying varying perspectives and increasing team effectiveness. Solutions to problems may be complex and take time to formulate. The management team members should each feel that the problems that exist are their problems, and that all participants have a vested interest in the solution.

Process of Dialogue

Dialogue should facilitate the team's effectiveness. Originally attributed to Socrates, dialogue has been used and expanded by many leadership authors. According to Senge (1990), physicist Bohm describes the process as follows, "Dialogue suggests a free flow of meaning between people." Further, the group accesses a larger pool of meaning that can't be accessed by individuals alone. Senge says the purpose of dialogue is to go beyond the understanding held by each person and to explore difficult issues from many points of view. Bohm identifies three conditions for real dialogue to occur:

1. All participants must suspend their assumptions both figuratively and literally and hold them in front of the group for all to see.
2. All must regard each other as colleagues.
3. A facilitator must be present.*

The steps in the dialogue process are as follows:

1. Suspend certainty about your beliefs.
2. Listen intently.

---

* The facilitator does not need to be a formal, high-paid consultant. (The role of the facilitator is most important when a team is first being formed, so need not be present indefinitely.) The role can be played by a member of the board, a skilled social worker, or another individual who is skilled in interpersonal relationships but who is not a member of the team.

3. Focus on understanding the others' point of view.
4. Listen to your listening (listen to what is going on in your head while you should be listening).
5. Clarify your own thinking.
6. Be honest.
7. Expect to feel uncomfortable.

Senge explains that a unique relationship develops among team members who enter into dialogue regularly. The technique of dialogue enables people to feel safe in the group, allows them to challenge existing processes, and, in fact, requires them to speak out. They learn how to listen, how to be honest with the group, how to identify biases that each person brings to the table, and how to trust. Over time, members of the executive management team learn the use of techniques that make them more effective and productive as a unit.

The dialogue approach can be used in identifying problems. "Identifying" the problem is the most difficult step in problem solving. The team offers an effective way to take a broad perspective in problem definition and solution.

STRUCTURE AND AUTHORITIES

The relationship of the management team within the organization should be articulated so that all staff can understand the team's responsibilities and authorities. The authorities of team members in relationship to department heads should also be explained. In some instances, the reporting relationship might be hierarchical and carry line authority; in others, it might be limited to a communications function. If an organization has several teams (e.g., executive management team, interdisciplinary clinical team, quality assurance team), the differences between the teams should be made quite clear.

Although a team enhances management, it should not replace the responsibilities of individuals. Individuals should remain responsible and accountable for the functions assigned to them. This should be made clear to team members, staff, and clients. Referral to "a team" should never be used as an excuse for a manager not to act on a problem brought forth by a client, a staff member, or a consultant.

MAJOR FUNCTIONS

Once formed, the executive management team (EMT) should be involved in a broad variety of activities. To have full impact upon the organization, the EMT should touch all the major management functions, including the following:

- Operations review
- Fiscal review and budgeting
- Quality assurance
- Human resources
- Regulation review and survey preparation
- Management communications

Operations review and overall organizational problem solving is arguably the single most important purpose of the team. Simply put, operations is performing the organization's core tasks effectively, and an effective management team will feel that they have a stake in almost every activity because they are a team.

Organizations face constant pressure to make decisions, to solve problems, and to move the organization forward. When major operational problems arise in LTC organizations, they are often solved through the eyes of one individual, the administrator or the CEO. Operations review by the management team means letting the team participate in analyzing the problem and recommending solutions. Often, the broader the solution to a problem, the more effective it will be for the long run. The culture must be established so that it does not detract from the CEO or any other team member to bring a problem to the group. This demonstration of trust and confidence in peer judgment strengthens the relationships among team members.

Fiscal review involves the EMT in overseeing the LTC organization's financial health. Revenue and expenditures should be compared to budget and, if necessary, short-term corrective actions taken. During annual budget preparation, the EMT can balance allocations across units, removing the onus from the CEO of unilaterally decreasing or increasing a given unit's budget. The EMT is also the body to consider new programs to generate revenue or new initiatives to cut costs.

The EMT members ultimately carry the burden of running the major functions of the organization within budget. The more that senior managers understand financial issues, the more they will be able to contribute to saving costs, generating revenue, or engaging in other initiatives.

Human resource issues are a constant challenge to LTC organizations. Many LTC organizations are small and do not have staff dedicated to human resource functions. Because workforce issues affect all units and all functions of an organization, they are important issues to address from an EMT approach.

The EMT should review all HR activities, including such issues as turnover rate, factors that inhibit or enhance retention and staff satisfaction, new hire policies, and continuing education. They can evaluate specific problems that are affecting a single unit, perhaps by relocating staff. The team should also be able to pose ideas on how to restructure, reengineer, or cross-train staff to provide greater strength, as well as expertise, in the LTC organization's manpower pool.

Regulation review and survey preparation can be divided and coordinated by a strong management team. Individuals can be assigned the responsibility for keeping up with certain regulatory areas—an overwhelming task for a single individual for many LTC services. Similarly, preparing for surveys can be coordinated by the EMT. A well-organized regulatory schedule with regular reporting and updates on new or revised regulations will promote smoother survey administration.

Communication is perhaps the most important function of the EMT. Most managers, when asked, believe they are effective communicators. Experience and informal surveys indicate that only about one-third of managers actually know how to communicate effectively on a consistent basis. For the management team to communicate effectively, training and guidance may be needed, something that can be gained through external consultants and through EMT members sharing techniques with each other. The EMT can also implement a strong communications program within the LTC organization, disseminating information with other mid-level managers, establishing a corporate culture of open communication, and ensuring that the organization employs a range of communication mechanisms.

SUMMARY

Teams can be an effective way to manage LTC operations, particularly because of the small number of managers in many LTC organizations. Collectively, team members bring a wealth of experience and a diversity of perspectives that can enhance problem solving and future planning. Especially in LTC organizations that have very shallow management staff, a team approach can strengthen management depth and expertise. However, implementing and maintaining teams requires work. An LTC organization that commits to using a team approach to management must allocate resources to support team activity and then will accrue the benefits.

KEYS TO MANAGEMENT SUCCESS

- Identify members of the executive management team based on the organization's major functions.

- Educate managers about *how* to work in teams.
- Allocate the time and resources required to educate the team and allow it to function.
- Use a facilitator when first creating a new management team and, if feasible, whenever a new member joins the team.
- Take a team approach to identifying problems.
- Empower the team to challenge existing processes by questioning why things are done as they are and to search out improved strategies.
- Structure EMT activities for comprehensive operations review on a regular basis, as well as to solve immediate problems.

REVIEW QUESTIONS

1. Name five benefits of using a management team.
2. List three barriers to using a management team.
3. Define the process of dialogue.
4. How can a facilitator empower a team to maximize its functioning?
5. Delineate the types of operational functions that an executive management team should review.

REFERENCES

Katzenbach, J. R., and D. K. Smith. 1993. *The Wisdom of Teams: Creating the High Performance Organization.* Boston: Harvard Business School Press.

Merriam-Webster's Collegiate Dictionary, 11th Edition. 2003. Springfield, MA: Merriam-Webster, Inc.

Senge, P. 1990. *The Fifth Discipline: The Art and Practice of the Learning Organization.* New York: Doubleday.

CHAPTER SIX

Financing

"Love may make the world go round,
but money turns the crank."

Unknown

The accountant was new to Community Social Services. She had never seen such a complicated set of accounts! The organization had multiple sources of revenue: a contract with the Area Agency on Aging to provide homemaker services, a grant from a local foundation to offer caregiver support, a subcontract with a medical group to provide mental health counseling for a managed care health plan, an endowment funded by donations from clients and families, and more. Expenditures were equally complex: full-time staff billed to several projects, contractors used only for specific services, in-kind contributions related to tax-exempt status, durable medical equipment purchased for clients from the endowment operating account, and so forth. Her first thought was to do a thorough analysis of the accounting programs to make sure all revenues and expenditures were being handled appropriately. But then a request came from the parent medical center: should they open an adult day center, either a social model or a health model? She was asked to determine the financial feasibility of this potential new service. They needed an answer within two weeks. Where to start?

THE FINANCING OF long-term care services is, if possible, even more complicated than the financing of acute and ambulatory care. Long-term care service financial management requires a number of challenging items:

- creative combining of multiple sources of funding;
- managing a variety of government programs, each with its own regulations and payment systems;
- collecting from a high percentage of private pay clients and families;
- mixing for-profit and not-for-profit business activities; and
- operating on slim margins.

Similar to acute and ambulatory care, long-term care providers face ever-evolving financial arrangements and the uneasy balancing of capitated managed care, fee-for-service, and case-based payment. Many long-term care agencies offer more than one type of service, compounding the complexity of managing financial operations within the organization. From the standpoint of the individual client, use of long-term care services is less predictable and more fragmented than acute care, making insurance and billing difficult.

From the national perspective, long-term care costs are a contradiction. Although spending does not begin to compare to the amount of funds spent for acute hospital care or physician care, the public and private funds spent for long-term care have been steadily increasing. As a nation, society regards long-term care as a personal or family responsibility. In reality, public programs pay for a considerable portion of long-term care. Continuity of client care across services is an oft-expressed goal, but the funding streams for long-term care are fraught with eligibility criteria that restrict access and inhibit continuity. In brief, achieving comprehensive financing of long-term care services is as complicated as attaining comprehensiveness and continuity in the array of services themselves.

This chapter summarizes national expenditures for long-term care and then addresses the basic financial framework that a manager needs to know to supervise the accounting department in handling revenues and expenditures. Knowledge of fiscal issues is also crucial to strategic planning and to analyzing new business opportunities and capital finance projects.

Table 6.1. Personal Healthcare Expenditures for Long-Term Care, 1960 and 2001 (in billions)

	1960		2001	
	Amount	*Percentage*	*Amount*	*Percentage*
TOTAL, All expenditures	$26.7	100	$1,424.5	100
Nursing facilities	0.8	3.00	98.9	6.94
Home care	0.1	0.37	33.2	2.33
Hospitals	9.2	34.46	451.2	31.67
Physicians	5.4	20.22	313.6	22.01
Other	11.2	41.95		

Source: Health US 2003, Table 115. 2003. Hyattsville, MD: US DHHS, National Center for Health Statistics.

MAJOR SOURCES OF REVENUE

In the data gathered by the federal government, no single category of spending is labeled "long-term care," and the absence of such explicit itemization makes it difficult to report national spending for long-term care. The data available at the national level report spending for nursing facilities and Medicare-certified home health agencies. These two categories are thus used as proxies for examining trends in long-term care spending.

Table 6.1 shows the amounts of personal healthcare expenditures spent for nursing facility care and home health care in 1960 and 2001. As is evident, in 1960, home health care barely appeared, and nursing home care was dwarfed by other categories. In the ensuing 40 years, the total amount of money spent each year on skilled nursing home care and Medicare-certified home care grew noticeably, in aggregate and on a per capita basis.

Government Sources of Funding

Table 6.2 gives examples of major government funding sources and the types of services they pay for.

Medicare, the nation's single largest payer for healthcare, does not technically pay for long-term care services. Medicare was created as a safety net to prevent older people or those with severe permanent disabilities from losing their life savings as the result of an acute illness. By legislative mandate, Medicare does not cover services for people who have maintenance-level chronic conditions. In practice, Medicare does cover select long-term care services on a very limited basis. For example, to receive care in a skilled nursing facility, a person must first be hospitalized for three days for an acute illness episode and have the potential for improvement. Once improvement has been maximized, Medicare will no longer pay.

The Medicare Prescription Drug, Improvement and Modernization Act of 2003 (MMA) created dramatic changes in the Medicare program, including the recognition that chronic conditions cannot be separated from the care for acute illnesses. MMA changed that payment system in some way for almost every type of Medicare provider, as well as changing the services covered. The long-term impact on long-term care clients and providers remains to be determined. As the MMA provisions take effect over the next few years, managers of most LTC organizations will be adapting their operations to accommodate new regulations, services, and payment procedures. Detailed information for providers is available on the CMS website, www.cms.gov. Services covered by Medicare and the annual deductible and co-pay amounts can be found in consumer-oriented format also at www.cms.gov.

Medicaid is the federal-state matching program that covers healthcare for those with low incomes. Medicaid was passed in 1965 as a companion to Medicare legislation. Each state establishes its own service array within the framework specified by the federal government. This means that each state has formulated its own set of services covered, eligibility criteria, and payment method. The callout

Table 6.2. Select Federal Programs Paying and the Services they Cover

Program	Services Covered
Medicare*	Skilled nursing care
	Home care
	Hospice care
	LTC hospital
	Rehabilitation therapies
	Mental health
Medicaid	Skilled nursing care
	Home care
	Hospice care
	Rehabilitation therapies
	Mental health care
	Adult day care
	Assisted living (some states only)
Veterans Affairs	Skilled nursing care
	Home care
	Hospice care
	Rehabilitation therapies
	Mental health care
	Adult day care
	Respite
Older Americans Act	Congregate meals
	Meals on Wheels
	Homemaker
	Case management
Title XX	Home care
	Chore service

*Assumes short-term prognosis of improvement.

box "Federal Medicaid Mandated and Optional Services" highlights the Medicaid array of services. Medicaid is the single largest payer for nursing home care and also covers home care and hospice. In some states, Medicaid covers adult day services, assisted living, and other long-term care services. The term *Medi-Medi* refers to clients who are eligible for both Medicare and Medicaid funds. Major drawbacks of Medicaid include the following: (1) establishing eligibility for a client may take up to six months, requiring providers to cover a considerable cash float; and (2) payment rates are low in many states. Accepting Medicaid payment thus often requires a provider to commit to volume to compensate for the regulatory requirements and low per-capita compensation.

Title XX of the Social Security Act provides block grants to states for health and social services. Each state determines how it will spend these funds. Title XX is used in many states for home support services, such as home health, homemaker, and chore service. The mechanism used to disburse Title XX funds within a state is also established by the state, resulting in considerable variation.

Older Americans Act (OAA) funds were authorized in 1965 at the same time as Medicare and Medicaid. They are administered by the Administration on Aging (AoA) and disbursed to states and local Area Agencies on Aging (AAA or Triple A). The OAA allocates funds for specific categories of services, with the total dollar amount given to a state calculated on the total population age 60 and older. How funds are distributed locally and at the state level depends on local decision making and a required periodic needs assessment. Programs funded are typically support services rather than direct healthcare. These include congregate meals, meals on wheels, case management, homemaker, chore service, money management, legal consultation, and caregiver support.

The U.S. Department of Veterans Affairs (VA) operates the largest healthcare system in the world. The VA offers a comprehensive array of services through each of its 163 medical centers. These include skilled nursing, hospice, home care, caregiver support, adult day services, and rehabilitation, among others. In locations where the

Federal Medicaid Mandated and Optional Services

Mandatory Services	Optional Services
Inpatient hospital services	Podiatrist services
Outpatient hospital services	Optometrists' services
Rural health clinic and federally qualified health center (FQHC) services	Psychologists' services
	Medical social worker services
	Private duty nursing
	Clinic services
	Physical therapy
Laboratory and x-ray services	Occupational therapy
	Speech, hearing, and language disorders
Nurse practitioners' services	Prescribed drugs
	Dentures
Nursing facility (NF) services and home health services for individuals age 21 and over	Prosthetic devices
	Screening services
	Preventive services
	Rehabilitative services
	Intermediate care facility—mental retardation services (ICF—MR)
Physician and dentist (medical and surgical services)	Nursing facility (NF) for individuals under 21
	Personal care services
	Transportation services
	Case management services
	Hospice care services
	Inpatient and NF services for individuals 65 and over in institutions for mental diseases

VA does not provide the service directly, it contracts with agencies in the community to provide care. Skilled nursing care and adult day care are frequent contract services. Those who use the VA system for care include a high proportion of people with chronic and disabling conditions. In addition to younger adults with disabilities, the VA serves many older adults. Other government programs that provide long-term care services directly or contract with others to provide services include worker's compensation, state and local mental health agencies, programs for the developmentally disabled, public housing, and sundry social services.

Private Sources of Funding

Private pay sources of funding for long-term care include the individual and family, private insurance (both commercial indemnity and health plan), and long-term care insurance. As noted above, although many government sources pay for some long-term care services, the burden of payment is primarily on the individual and family.

Long-term care insurance has grown markedly during the past few years. LTC insurance has been available since the early 1980s, but public perception of its availability is relatively recent. The benefit structure of LTC insurance policies and the rates have become more attractive in recent years, and the marketing has become more aggressive. Figure 6.1 shows the increase in number of policies sold nationally.

LTC insurance policies vary in the services covered, but typically include skilled nursing and home care. Many of the newer benefit structures include adult day services and assisted living, or a lump-sum payout that the beneficiary can spend on whatever assistance he or she chooses. For many policies, eligibility for benefits is based on ADL limits rather than, or in conjunction with, diagnosis. Individual service providers can make arrangements with long-term care insurance companies on a case-specific basis to cover the care for an individual or in advance to cover a group of individuals, such as residents of a continuing care retirement community.

Commercial indemnity insurance typically covers long-term care services that mirror Medicare in paying for services for people with a temporary condition and a diagnosis of expected improvement. LTC services covered within limits may include skilled nursing care for a limited period of time, rehabilitation, mental health care, home

Figure 6.1. Growth in Number of Long-Term Care Insurance Policies Sold (in thousands)

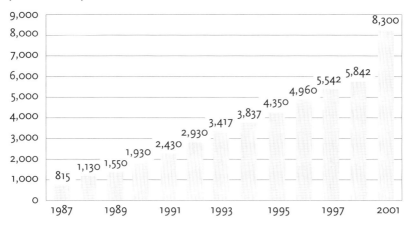

Source: Coronel, S. 2000. *Research Findings: Long-Term Care Insurance in 1997–98*, Figure 1, p. 14. Washington, DC: Health Insurance Association of America. Updated November 2003 from www.hiaa.org. Used with permission.

care, and hospice. Maintenance and social support services are seldom covered.

Managed care coverage of long-term care is minimal. Medicare+ Choice plans, for those age 65 and older, have the limitations of Medicare. Although almost all enrollees have some type of chronic illness by virtue of age, Medicare was not intended to cover long-term care. Medicare managed care plans may cover more services than fee-for-service Medicare, such as vision and hearing care, but do not cover personal care or skilled care on a maintenance basis. The Social HMOs (S/HMOs) and PACE, the Program of All-Inclusive Care for the Elderly, are exceptions in that they do cover long-term care services on a select basis. These programs are highly limited in their geographic availability, with fewer than 30 total sites nationwide.

Individuals and families are major payers for almost all types of LTC care services. Private pay by individuals and families is difficult to quantify at the national level, but for many long-term care providers, it is the largest single source of payment. For example, the nation had approximately 12,250 private home health agencies in

2002, compared to about 7,700 Medicare-certified home care agencies. Although these private agencies may bill several sources of payment, individuals and families who pay for care directly are likely to be the core of their business. Similarly, about one-third of the billions spent annually on nursing home care is paid for by individuals. Until recently, assisted living and congregate housing for seniors was paid for exclusively by individuals, and individuals remain the largest single payer source.

Payment Systems

Through the Balanced Budget Act of 1997, Medicare attempted to curtail spending for long-term care by implementing case-based reimbursement for several major long-term care services. Table 6.3 shows payment systems for select long-term care services. Medicare developed a different client assessment and payment method for each service. These are all based on some combination of functional status assessment and diagnosis, but each uses a different measure of functional status and different diagnostic codes. These radical changes in Medicare payment pose significant challenges for LTC provider organizations.

Even though an organization might have only a small proportion of Medicare clients, the entire organization must comply. Nursing homes are an example. The MDS (minimum data set) required by Medicare must be completed for all residents, even though the number of Medicare-certified beds may be fewer than the facility's number of non-certified beds.

Multiple government funding sources also mean compliance with multiple sets of regulations and billing systems. For example, a large healthcare system that has acute care, skilled nursing, and home care must be able to manage the DRG, MDS/RUGS, and OASIS/Home Care payment systems. A patient who receives care from all three of these services must be assessed under all three assessment methodologies.

Table 6.3. Medicare Prospective Payment System, by Service

LTC Service	Payment System	Assessment
Hospitals	DRGs	DRG
Rehabilitation	CMGs	IRF
Nursing facilities	RUGS	MDS
Hospice care	4 levels of care, fixed per level Capped, amount set annually	Prognosis of 6 months or less*
Home care	HHRGs	OASIS
Long-term care hospitals	LTCH-DRGs	DRG
Psychiatric hospitals	IPF	†

*Assessment tool based on organizational locus of hospice.
†Assessment tool not determined as of June 2004.

Notes: CMG = case mix group; RUGS = resource utilization groups; IRF = functional independence measure; MDS = minimum data set; OASIS = outcomes assessment information system; HHRG = home health related groups; IPF = inpatient psychiatric facilities

Most long-term care services combine multiple sources of funding. Table 6.4 shows examples of the funding sources of select services. To compound dealing with multiple sources, funding is more fragmented and depends on payers less stable than Medicare. For organizations that offer several types of services, each service may have different payment streams that must be billed. Compliance with the care and financial regulations for all these sources of funding must also be managed by the LTC provider.

Care provision is affected by the amount of payment, the payment system, and the payment process. Managers must continuously monitor the different methods of payment and determine how to provide quality patient services within the current framework. Management must also anticipate new methods of payment and be prepared to adjust the provision of services to maximize client care and profitability.

Table 6.4. Potential Payers for Select Long-Term Care Services

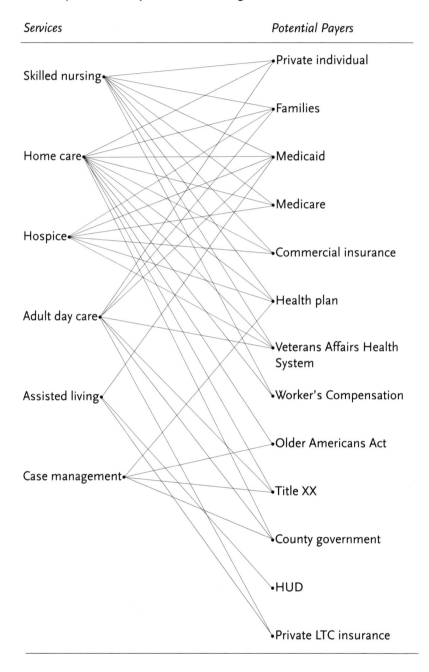

Services

Potential Payers

Skilled nursing

Home care

Hospice

Adult day care

Assisted living

Case management

Private individual

Families

Medicaid

Medicare

Commercial insurance

Health plan

Veterans Affairs Health System

Worker's Compensation

Older Americans Act

Title XX

County government

HUD

Private LTC insurance

MAJOR EXPENDITURES

LTC is a very labor-intensive business, and, consequently, labor is the single greatest expense for LTC service providers. For many LTC organizations, labor represents two-thirds to three-fourths of the operating budget. Labor costs are fixed to the extent that staff are regular employees. Some LTC organizations, such as private home care agencies, use registry personnel, so they can add staff when volume is high but do not carry the fixed expense when volume is low. "Flex staffing" is also used, which enables employers to send staff home if client volume is low.

Salaries are typically set by the local market. Professional or trade associations may conduct a wage and benefit analysis annually, thereby enabling the LTC organization to compare its salaries to the market. Benefits packages vary widely, and many LTC organizations do not offer strong benefit packages due to the low profit margins. States specify some salary and benefit parameters, such as worker's compensation insurance or caps on the wage component of Medicaid rates, that directly or indirectly limit salaries.

Supplies are another large routine expenditure. LTC organizations may achieve significant discounts on everything from clinical supplies to office supplies by belonging to a group purchasing entity. LTC organizations that belong to large vertical or horizontal healthcare systems may receive these discounts through contracts negotiated by the corporate office. Others may find group purchasing arrangements through trade associations.

In recent years, insurance has become a large expenditure for all healthcare providers. The LTC organization may have no control over insurance costs, as the rates are set by the state or by insurance companies that offer few choices. Shopping around, joining an insurance pool offered by a trade association, or self-insuring are all options to consider. However, the effective manager must consider insurance a major expenditure, along with labor and supplies.

FINANCE OPERATIONS

An LTC provider must have standard operating procedures in place for handling all aspects of financing and must have staff dedicated exclusively to managing finances. In large organizations, this may be an entire department with a large staff and a sophisticated electronic data processing system. In a small organization, this might be a contract with an accounting firm for oversight and clerical staff for day-to-day processing. Accounting software is readily available to facilitate standard accounting functions, and specialty software has been developed to enable organizations to comply with specific government programs. The challenge is to know how to select reliable software products and how to work with accountants, whether in-house or on contract.

Whatever the day-to-day arrangements, finance is an integral component of management and one that cannot be delegated to the chief financial officer or contract accountant exclusively. All managers must comprehend and be comfortable handling financial issues affecting the organization including operations processes, productivity, budgeting, and financial statement review. Using the executive management team described in Chapter 5 or establishing a finance committee can help bring key managers together to address major financial issues and related problems. Additionally, all staff must be educated about the financial implications of clinical care. Billing must be coded appropriately, and clinical staff must accurately record the services they perform so that billing reflects actual care and the associated expenses.

Most managers should have formal training in basic accounting and be familiar with income statements and balance sheets. All senior managers should know the basic statistics for the organization's revenue generation and expenditures (e.g., who is the best payer and what are the largest fixed and variable costs). The organization should establish fixed processes for budgeting, paying salaries, handling accounts receivable and accounts payable, and other routine financial activities. Larger LTC organizations or those that are part of large corporations are likely to have financial systems in place. Small providers, or new ones, will need to hire external consultants to establish standard business financial functions, and then hire dedicated personnel as the organization expands or maintain relationships for contractual assistance. Periodic audit, even for family-owned proprietary businesses, is necessary to ensure that all financial affairs are being handled appropriately at all levels of the organization.

Budgeting is essential for all organizations, even small family-owned businesses. Most organizations prepare a budget annually. The process of preparing the budget can be used to strengthen the organizational commitment of staff and managers. Managers and staff can be asked their preferences for spending as inputs to the initial drafting of the budget and/or asked to review and comment on a draft. Negotiating cuts or compromises, if needed, during the budget process, results in buy-in to the final budget and the performance expectations inherent in the annual budget. The financial performance expected of each unit then becomes easier to achieve, since managers and staff have basically agreed to expectations as part of the budgeting process.

Managing the Accounting

As described above, LTC services rely on a great number of payers. Diligent administrators can find pockets of funds for long-term care services from many federal, state, county, and local government sources, as well as from a myriad of private sources. The challenge then becomes dealing with the multiple contracts, payment systems, reporting requirements, eligibility requirements, and other regulations. Some, such as Medicare, require electronic billing, with proper coding of client condition and compliance with numerous other regulations.

In addition to collecting revenue from formal organizations, the LTC organization must collect payment from individuals and families. The need to interact with several dozen families and clients each month can bring emotional, as well as financial, challenges. Individuals frail enough to need long-term care may have any number of problems that make it difficult for them to pay their bill each month. And, each person has a personal story. It's much easier to negotiate with an objective third-party payer who operates a business 9 a.m. to 5 p.m. than to deal with a distraught individual or family who may be hard to find, have a heart-wrenching story, or challenge why care costs so much.

Fortunately, with today's advanced information systems, accounting packages are readily available that will perform revenue collection tasks to the specification of the payer. The task of the LTC manager is to evaluate or select an automated accounting system and external accountant or auditor that will ensure correct procedures are used and accurate reports produced. Vendors with a track record of good service and strong company stability should be selected. Then, the LTC manager's task is to monitor the accounting department and regularly—weekly or monthly—review the financial performance of the organization to be sure that revenues are being collected and bills paid on a timely basis with minimal problems.

Operating on Tight Budgets

The operating margins for long-term care services vary widely. Some long-term care services, like adult day care, consistently depend on grants and donations from individuals and community agencies to stay solvent. In contrast, assisted living and skilled nursing facilities are often owned by for-profit companies and must generate income for stockholders. In general, profit margins in long-term care are quite low, and lower than any other component of the healthcare industry. This puts pressure on managers, as there is only a small financial cushion. It also means little money is available with which to experiment, try new things, or be creative. Many staff are hired at low or minimum wage, resulting in higher net revenues perhaps, but also causing staff turnover and lack of expertise, which

Table 6.5. Sources of Capital For Long-Term Care Organizations

For-profit organizations	Equity market (stocks)
	Reinvestment of capital gains and profit
	Fund-raising (not tax deductible)
	Loans (commercial)
Not-for-profit organizations	Bond market
	Reinvestment of net revenue
	Fund-raising (tax-deductible)
	Loans (government-backed)

may ultimately cost the organization more than paying more for better-trained staff.

In brief, the tight financial performance of most long-term care providers requires managers to be skillful at managing not only money, but all other aspects of the organization.

CAPITAL FINANCE

Despite being labor-intensive, all LTC organizations require capital at some point to fund space, renovation or construction, and equipment, both clinical and administrative. Sources of capital depend in part on the tax status of the organization (see Table 6.5). For-profit organizations can offer stock or retain dividends and capital gains to raise needed capital. Not-for-profit organizations can seek bond support from local government authorities or reinvest net gain on operations (i.e., profit). Both can engage in fund-raising and seek private donors. Loans are probably the most common source of capital. These can be acquired from independent sources, such as local banks. For some long-term care services, such as assisted living or senior housing, certain government programs such as the Department of Housing and Urban Development (HUD) offer loan programs.

For stand-alone organizations that do not have a corporate headquarters to turn to, state and national trade associations are perhaps the best sources of information on how to raise capital. Those organizations that have boards are well-advised to have financial experts as board members. Organizations that belong to large corporations should find experts on capital at the corporate level.

Every organization should anticipate its capital needs through its strategic planning (see Chapter 7) and should plan for routine replacement by regularly funding a depreciation account.

SUMMARY

Long-term care financing comes from an array of different government and private sources. LTC organizations must be creative in combining funds from these multiple sources, but must be diligent in complying with the financial, reporting, and regulatory requirements of each funder. Before accepting a new funding source, the LTC organization must consider the inherent operating requirements. Accounting functions can be handled by automated programs to a large extent, but management staff must choose the information systems and monitor the LTC organization's financial status on a regular basis. Given the tight budget of most LTC organizations, staff in all departments must be aware of the financial realities of their business and thus share the responsibility for preparing and managing according to an annual budget.

KEYS TO MANAGEMENT SUCCESS

- For each LTC service offered, explore all possible funding sources.
- For each funding source, know its accounting requirements and service compliance regulations before agreeing to accept

the payment source. Train all staff to understand and use proper coding.

- Develop or purchase accounting software that automates processing as much as possible.
- Select vendors with experience, a track record, and the stability to be there in the future.
- Train all managers to understand major expenditures and monitor spending according to budget.
- Prepare an annual budget, with input from managers and staff.
- Plan well in advance for capital expenditures and finance capital separately from operations.

REVIEW QUESTIONS

1. What are five major sources of payment for long-term care services?
2. What is the official policy of the Medicare program regarding payment for long-term care?
3. What is the role of Medicaid in paying for long-term care services?
4. What are sources of capital for long-term care organizations?
5. What is the easiest way to comply with accounting regulations required by each provider source?
6. How do long-term care services compare to acute care in terms of numbers and types of payer sources?

CHAPTER SEVEN

Strategic Planning

"He turns not back who is bound to a star."

Leonardo da Vinci (1452–1519)

The Visiting Nurse Association (VNA) was worried. The number of clients served seemed to dwindle each month. Another hospital had purchased a Medicare-certified home care agency that could not on its own accommodate the change in Medicare reimbursement methodology. That agency had always been a competitor, but in a slightly different geographic service area. Now, competition from the agency was stronger as it encroached on the VNA's service area. Furthermore, losing the hospital as a referral base was devastating. Between hospital agencies and managed care, the VNA was being squeezed out of clients who had choices. Moreover, it was increasingly difficult to hire nurses and nurses' aides. The national nursing shortage had finally hit the VNA's metropolitan area, and the state budget crunch had resulted in a paring back of the nurse aide training program offered at the local junior college. The VNA wondered if it should just downsize its operation, and thereby need fewer staff for fewer clients, borrow money and aggressively expand to counter the competition, or just close its doors and quit.

STRATEGIC PLANNING IS the process of determining the organization's goals, measurable objectives, and direction for the immediate future, as well as reaffirming the organization's mission and long-range vision. No organization can survive without a plan or sense of direction. The purpose of having a strategic plan is to provide a basis for daily decision making and resource allocation: A strategic plan focuses the organization on its priority business strategies and helps managers align on important issues. It ensures that the organization continues to fulfill its mission despite environmental changes and an evolving business climate. The process of creating the plan builds consensus and buy-in among the organization's stakeholders, including community members and staff.

Major healthcare systems have engaged in strategic planning for so many years that most have a well-defined internal process for doing so. In contrast, many long-term care organizations do not have this tradition. Long-term care organizations have not had the same external pressures warranting selective positioning in the marketplace; and many do not have the internal resources to devote to "planning" rather than daily operations. In the future, as the field of long-term care becomes more complex and more competitive, strategic planning will be imperative. The purpose of this chapter is to provide an overview of the strategic planning process.

PARTICIPANTS

Strategic planning is a process whereby the organization determines where it will go in the near-term future—two to three years—while keeping its sight on its long-term mission. For the ultimate plan to be adopted by the organization, the process must involve formal and informal leaders throughout to gain their commitment and to craft a single vision reflecting diverse perspectives. In large organizations in a complex environment, the process takes six months to a year. In smaller organizations in less complex markets, a shorter time frame is possible.

Strategic planning begins by naming a task force of key stakeholders who will meet throughout the process. Some will have an active role in gathering and interpreting information. The major contribution of other members will be to convey information to their peers and constituents. The board and external stakeholders are involved to reaffirm commitment to the organization. A critical outcome of strategic planning is developing consensus and commitment among all involved with the organization's future direction.

In a large organization, a vice president or director of strategic planning would spearhead the process. In an LTC organization, which probably has a modest management staff, the strategic planning task force might well be led by the CEO. Members of the task force might be the executive management team, if one has been established (see Chapter 5) or, if not, might include the director of finance, the director of clinical or residential services, the person responsible for marketing or admissions, a representative of board or corporate headquarters, and a representative of the staff. Others throughout the organization may be brought in to assist with specific components of the plan. At the outset of the process, a timetable should be established to let everyone know what will be happening when.

BENEFITS

Strategic planning can be a long, sometimes tedious, and expensive process. Why should organizations bother? As noted above, the strategic plan provides the organization with a clear statement of where it is going and thus with the criteria for making decisions on a day-to-day basis. The organization is prepared for the future, rather than passively continuing its activities and failing to evolve to meet a changing environment. The benefits of strategic planning include the following:

- The organization's vision and mission are reaffirmed or revised.
- The client population is characterized in detail (otherwise, this may not be done on a regular basis).
- The competition is analyzed in a comprehensive manner.
- A focus is provided for decision making and resource allocation.

Figure 7.1. The Components of the Strategic Planning Process

- Management leaders participate in shaping the future of the organization and thus become stronger leaders.
- Employees understand the rationale for decisions and their role in the organization's future.

BASIC COMPONENTS

The basic steps in strategic planning are presented in Figure 7.1.

Articulate Vision and Mission

The strategic planning process begins with articulating the organization's vision and mission. In most organizations, the staff and clients can tell you what the organization does—but in their own words and from the perspective of their interaction and roles with the organization. The vision and mission statements should be clearly and concisely articulated so that they are easy to communicate to all stakeholders, including staff, clients, professionals, and the community.

The vision statement (see sample vision statement) tells where the organization sees itself in the future. It is more global in nature than the mission statement.

The mission is a short, explicit statement (see sample mission statements) that encompasses the goals and activities of the organization. The mission should be shared with the staff and inculcated into their daily practice. All staff should be able to cite the organization's mission and know how their jobs relate to its accomplishment.

The strategic planning process provides the opportunity to revisit both the vision and mission statements and to reaffirm or modify them. Many LTC organizations that are small, proprietary operations or are mandated government agencies may have been established without a vision or mission statement articulated—the vision may exist only in the head of the boss! The strategic planning process presents the opportunity to create these tools if they do not yet exist. They become valuable communication tools to develop the commitment of staff, clients, and colleagues. The strategic plan should guide the organization in accomplishing its mission and, ultimately, its vision. If these three organizational tools are not in alignment, something needs to change!

This is also the point at which the organization affirms its core business. This may be defined as a single service (e.g., to provide adult day services) or in a broader sense (e.g., to provide supportive housing to frail seniors at the level most appropriate for their needs). The core business should be consistent with the mission and support the long-term vision.

Define the Customers

The data components of a strategic plan begin with clearly defining the target population the organization currently serves and the population it desires to serve. Note that these two may be different. Detailed information is then gathered about the target population(s).

Long-term care is a service business: it exists to provide care to individuals. It's essential that the organization knows who these

Sample Vision Statement

Veterans Affairs Long Beach Healthcare System
Our vision is to be the preferred healthcare provider for veterans by exceeding their expectations and being recognized for quality care, innovation, and value.

VA Long Beach Healthcare System, 2003

Sample Mission Statements

Retirement Housing Foundation
The mission of Retirement Housing Foundation, a non-profit organization, is to provide a range of housing options and services for older adults, economically disadvantaged families, and persons with disabilities, according to their needs, in an environment enhancing the quality of life as it relates to their physical, mental, and spiritual well-being. Retirement Housing Foundation is committed to serving its residents and their local communities.

Retirement Housing Foundation, 2004

Providence Mount St. Vincent
The Providence Mount St. Vincent in West Seattle offers older adults a loving home during the transition from independence to increasing reliance on the services, support, and compassion of others. We are committeed to providing a caring service that respects the personal values and dignity of each individual.

The Sisters of Providence Health System continues the healing ministry of Jesus in the world of today, with special concern for those who are poor and vulnerable.

Working with others in a spirit of loving service, we strive to meet the health needs of people as they journey through life.

Providence Mount St. Vincent Health System, 2004

people are. In today's highly competitive world, with highly regulated and segmented financing, all internal operations and all external communications should be focused on the target audience. Organizations that don't know who their market is or don't know their market well are those that are most likely to get into trouble spending time and resources on non-essential activities.

Ask a family member of a client whom the organization serves in the community and they can probably give you a general answer: old people, poor families, people with HIV, etc. Most clients don't know exactly what an organization does, or all that it does, until they need services for themselves or for their family members. Ask a staff member whom an organization serves and all but the most sophisticated managers will tell you about their own clients and those served by their own department. In brief, whom an organization serves may not be a secret, but, unless the data are examined purposefully and comprehensively, it may not be obvious.

Data on clients should include information on demographic/economic status, insurance source, geographic residence, functional and diagnostic status, and utilization of services. Data come from an array of different sources. Compiling this information is one of the most labor- and time-intensive components of the plan. Secondary data can be compiled from many public sources, as well as proprietary ones. In addition, collecting primary data may be necessary for the organization to obtain the information needed for its plan. In addition to objective information, subjective information may be sought through surveys, interviews, or focus groups.

Demographic information on clients should include data pertaining to the characteristics that are related to health status and to service use or demand. Essential data on clients are as follows:

- Age
- Gender
- Family status
- Ethnicity/race

- Economic status
- Insurance status
- Geographic residence

Other desirable information on clients includes the following items:

- Functional status: ADLs, IADLs
- Diagnosis: physical
- Diagnosis: mental
- Chronic conditions
- Service utilization, current and past
- Recent admissions/discharges

The information must be gathered, analyzed, and distilled for the strategic planning task force to use in making decisions. As shown in Table 7.1, data come from a variety of sources, and the information available is not always in the desired format. This means manipulating the available information so that data from different sources are as comparable as possible.

Data can be presented in tables, charts, graphs, and maps to make it easy for all members of the strategic planning task force and stakeholders to understand. The task force may also ask for several iterative rounds of data before they are confident that they know enough to commit the organization to serving a certain target audience. The data may also contain surprises: even senior managers may not have realized that the geographic service area had shifted, or that the average age of clients had gradually climbed.

Analyze the External Market

The strategic plan must also examine the external marketplace so that the organization can determine its strengths and weaknesses compared to others and identify opportunities and threats for the

Table 7.1. Data Used for Strategic Planning and Sample Data Sources

Type of Informaton	Data Sources
Internal	
Client demographics	Admissions forms; special and routine reports
Client geographic location	Census data; discharge records
Client functional status	MDS; OASIS; other assessment data
Client diagnoses	Client clinical records
Utilization data	Special and routine reports
Community preferences	Focus groups; community surveys
Client preferences	Surveys—mail or telephone; client satisfaction questionnaires
Client referral source	Admissions forms
External	
Population location	Census data; maps
Community demographics	Census data; maps
Unmet needs	Area Agency on Aging 5-year plan; United Way; other local agencies
Utilization	State departments of health, social services, and mental health
Diagnosis prevalence	State departments of health, social services, and mental health
Competitor profile	Marketing materials; licensing agencies
Competitor location	Map
Collaborator profile	Marketing materials, licensing agencies
Collaborator location	Map
Collaborator utilization	Internal referral data

future. Similar to the internal data analysis, this requires gathering information from various places and putting together the pieces of the puzzle to achieve a comprehensive picture of the marketplace.

Without the strategic planning process, this thorough analysis of the competition and the collaborators is not typically done by an organization. Staff might know from experience who refers to them, who they refer to, and who the competition is, but this is not likely to be quantified on a regular basis or compared from service to service. Table 7.2 shows a highly condensed version of the type of information to be compared about collaborators and competitors.

Collaborators are organizations that can be worked with on a formal or informal basis. Relationships may already exist and be part of the LTC organization's strengths. Conversely, developing new relationships may be part of the strategic plan.

Environmental trends should also be considered. These should include an analysis of financing (new federal or state payment systems, arrival or closure of health plans); changing organizational relationships (opening of a new assisted living facility as a new corporate chain moves to town); and the advent of new regulations at federal, state, or local levels. Referral patterns, both those determined by physicians and those based on managed care contracts, are an important element of this analysis.

Knowing the competitors' clients may appear in both components of the plan: analyzing competitor clients may show community need pertinent to defining the client population and may also show competition and what must be done to move clients from the competitor organization to the LTC organization developing the strategic plan.

Evaluate Internal Resources

As an organization evaluates how it is meeting its current service commitments and considers changes in service, knowing the base

Table 7.2. Example of Competitor and Collaborator Home Care Agency Analysis

Name	Type of Services	Type of Clients	Service Area	Similarities	Differences
VNA Home Health	Skilled	Medicare	All of city		
Community Home Care	Skilled	Medicare	North city	Uses same physicians	Service area
Care at Home, Inc.	Personal care	Managed care contracts	Central city	Marketing materials confuse clients	No skilled services; no Medicare
Home Helpers	Homemaker	Private pay	All of city	Overlap of clients; same geography	No skilled services; no Medicare

of internal resources is critical. An organization cannot offer services or products without the internal capabilities to do so. These capabilities include staff, physical plant, capital, and other resources.

Staff

For LTC organizations, the most significant resource is people—as many as necessary and with the needed skill sets. In many areas of the country, registered nurses, personal care staff, and select types of therapists are in short supply. A new service can't be started if the people required to provide it are not available. Conversely, if the LTC organization has staff with rare expertise, this presents an opportunity that competing organizations might not be able to match.

Physical plant resources

To offer a new service, the appropriate space must be available. A skilled nursing facility might consider opening an Alzheimer's unit in a community where this is absent and clearly in demand. However, unless the facility has a unit of the desired size that can be locked, an enclosed garden for wanderers, and a separate activities space, the service might not be realistic.

Capital and start-up funds

Developing a new program or improving an existing one may require an infusion of funds. The LTC organization needs to evaluate its capability of acquiring these funds from any of the variety of sources.

Other resources

Resources that should be considered include reputation, current services that might be a referral base, current services that are under- or over-utilized, geographic location, and relationships either already in place or with the potential to develop.

Sample SWOT Analysis

Strengths	Excellent staff, strong reputation, capacity availabile
Weaknesses	Need to seek start-up funds, need to market to new target audience with no prior history with the organization
Opportunities	Contracts with hospitals, managed care organizations, or government agencies
Threats	Additional hospital-based home care opening

Complete SWOT Analysis

SWOT stands for strengths, weaknesses, opportunities, and threats. Once an organization has compiled data on the internal operations and external markets and forces, all the information is brought together so that the organization can evaluate the service and market niches that offer the greatest chance for success.

Strengths include a delineation of the LTC organization's current services, staff, physical facilities, financial status, reputation, and referral patterns. *Weaknesses* look at the same factors from the opposite perspective.

Opportunities and *threats* refer to the marketplace. Opportunities may be short-term and based on upcoming changes in contracts or government regulations or payment systems. Threats are the converse: opportunities that may be seized by the competition, or short-term opportunities that, if not taken, will be unavailable in the future. For example: Getting in with a new health plan as their preferred provider is a one-time opportunity. Once established, the relationship could continue indefinitely. If lost to a competitor, gaining the contract in the future might be quite challenging.

The SWOT analysis (see boxed example) concludes with laying out the LTC organization's strategic options for action. One future path may stand out or several alternatives may be offered, with the benefits and drawbacks of each articulated and supported by information.

Delineate Goals and Determine Measurable Objectives

Based on the above analysis, the organization determines its strategic direction and operationalizes this as goals for the future, typically over two to three years. The goals combine target population, core businesses, detailed services, competitive position, and collaborating organizations. Goals may be programmatic or financial, or involve service utilization, performance, client satisfaction, or another aspect. Goals should have explicit activities or accomplishments specified as objectives. Whereas goals might be expressed for a period of one to three years, *objectives* are shorter-term, smaller, and involve more discrete tasks that produce measurable results. Examples are shown in the callout box, "Sample Goals and Objectives."

Strategies and tactics will be developed by sub-groups within the organization to accomplish the objectives, and ultimately, the goals (see boxed example). *Strategies* are methods for accomplishing the objectives, and *tactics* are smaller, more refined activities that contribute to strategies.

Communicate

All of the stakeholders of the organization, including staff, should be informed about the strategic plan on a regular basis. The strategic plan may be developed by a small group: an executive management committee, a small strategic planning task force, or an external consultant. However, all stakeholders should be aware at the outset that the organization is undergoing a strategic planning process and should be involved in a positive way in gathering relevant data needed for the plan. Periodic updates may be provided

---

Sample Goal and Objectives

Goal: Increase client volume through contracting.

Objective 1: Seek at least two new contracts per year with managed care health plans.

Strategy: Offer new services that standard home care agencies don't have.

Tactic: Initiate new-baby post-delivery follow-up home visit.

Objective 2: Seek contracts with government agencies; at a minimum, have one completed in Year 1.

Strategy: Develop new services for new target audiences.

Tactic: Bring psychiatric nurse onto registry and seek contract with county mental health agency.

---

through verbal or written media, especially for the corporate office, board of directors, or owner. When the plan is finished, staff and stakeholders should be informed of the general outcomes, as well as the details as appropriate for their role with the organization.

Depending upon the size of the LTC organization, communication means could include a series of meetings with staff, board, and senior managers; articles in staff or shareholder newsletters; or a special report broadly or selectively distributed. Throughout the process, input should be solicited from stakeholders because the plan's implementation will ultimately depend on them.

Develop Action Plan with Responsibilities and Timetables

A final step of the plan, once approved by all of the stakeholders, is to add specific tasks, designate people responsible for each, and delineate a time frame. This should occur after the directions indicated by the plan have been approved by the board or corporate office, and after the direction has been communicated broadly to stakeholders. In that way, commitment to act will already have been made by those who are assigned tasks or others who may be affected by task activities.

The executive management team or senior managers should assume major roles in implementing the strategic plan. Progress toward the plan should be monitored on a regular basis, perhaps quarterly, and reported to stakeholders. Even if the plan is for three years, major strides toward goal achievement should be made within one year.

SUMMARY

Every LTC organization needs to have a plan for the future. In contrast to 30 years ago, when utilization was high and payment predictable, the current LTC environment is highly competitive and changes rapidly. An organization weathers unexpected changes in the environment better when it has a clear vision of its ultimate purpose and a plan in place to achieve this. This combination of underlying stability and strategic positioning is accomplished through the strategic planning process.

Strategic planning has a defined process and specific components. Depending upon the resources the organization has available, the plan can be done by a relatively small number of internal staff or external consultants, but all stakeholders should be aware of the process and the results. Small LTC organizations can expect to spend about six months gathering all the relevant information and completing the analysis; larger organizations might take up to a year.

Once formulated, the strategic plan facilitates organizational decision making so that resources are allocated to priority areas. Strategic plans are typically revisited at least every three years, to accomodate environmental and internal changes.

KEYS TO MANAGEMENT SUCCESS

- Be proactive in directing the organization's future.
- Reaffirm the organization's vision and mission.
- Engage in a strategic planning process, even if it is done on a small scale.
- Set measurable goals and objectives to guide performance, including timetable and responsiblities.
- Involve a broad array of stakeholders in developing the strategic plan and communicate progress regularly.

REVIEW QUESTIONS

1. What is the purpose of strategic planning?
2. What are the components of a strategic plan?
3. Why is stakeholder involvement essential?
4. What value are vision and mission statements to an organization?
5. What are the elements of a SWOT analysis?
6. What are the benefits of strategic planning?

CHAPTER EIGHT

Marketing

"Half the money I spend on advertising is wasted;
the trouble is I don't know which half."

John Wanamaker (1838–1922)

The 200-bed public nursing home was suffering from low occupancy of residents in need of skilled nursing. Administrators decided to convert one wing to assisted living, enabling it to serve an additional target population and access a different source of state funds. In the same small community, the Native American assisted living facility, touted as a model for cultural sensitivity, was having trouble recruiting residents, so they decided to explore licensing one wing as a skilled nursing facility, thereby building a steadier stream of occupants and a predictable payment source, Medicaid. Capital for the needed structural modifications was available from an earmarked fund, so money for physical plant adaptations would not be a barrier. A new adult day health center had just opened, providing a daytime site for people who might otherwise need to go to skilled nursing or assisted living. The director of the city's leading home care program threw up her hands! How could all these organizations think they would find enough clients in this small town? She knew that her agency was highly experienced at keeping very ill people at home, and her organization had a longstanding reputation with the community's hospital discharge planner. She was confident that she would continue to capture this business—but, she was also a little anxious about the sudden fierce competition for a relatively small market.

WHAT CAN WE do to assure ourselves that our decisions to expand or develop a new business line will be successful?

Marketing is a relatively new phenomenon to the healthcare field. For years, healthcare organizations were fully occupied and were not hurting financially, and marketing was often viewed as somehow unethical or inappropriate. The radical changes in the healthcare environment over the past 30 years have changed that view, and marketing is now considered an essential management function.

LTC organizations have lagged behind acute hospitals and health plans. As recently as 1980, nursing homes were almost fully occupied, hospice was just a nascent concept, adult day centers were sparse, and home care was primarily offered through public health departments and the visiting nurses associations (VNAs). During the past 25 years, LTC organizations of all types have proliferated, while payment and regulatory changes have restricted operations. Thus, marketing has now become essential to LTC organizations. This chapter presents the basic concepts of marketing that must be woven together to develop an effective marketing plan.

DEFINITION AND FRAMEWORK

Marketing is the "process of facilitating the exchange between two parties wishing to complete a transaction for goods and/or services." The transaction benefits each party and is based on agreement of product, price, and distribution.

The Four Ps

A now-traditional marketing framework defines the four Ps of marketing: product, place, price, and promotion. This means having the product, price, promotion, and place of distribution effectively in place to effect a beneficial exchange between the parties. The task of the LTC organization is to plan, identify, and communicate how the exchange will take place in the most efficient and mutually beneficial manner.

The four Ps are elaborated as follows:

1. ***Product***. This is the service or product offered to the client. It must be defined so that the client believes that this is the product he or she wants; that it meets a perceived need; and that it has the desired characteristics. For LTC organizations, the product is typically a service—some combination of health, social, and functional support services. Consumer research may have been conducted by the LTC organization or other party to indicate that clients are willing, interested, and inclined to buy this product/service.
2. ***Price***. This relates to the economic value placed on the services or product being offered. The product or service may be price sensitive or not, depending on the type of clients served and the competition. In long-term care, private pay can be a major payer, and thus the price can vary greatly depending upon what private individuals can and are willing to pay. In contrast, Medicaid is also a large payer for select LTC services, but many states set rates artificially and make prices very inelastic.
3. ***Place***. This refers to where the product or service will be available for clients and how it will be distributed. Place generally refers to distribution channels and methods of consumer buying. For an LTC organization, the place of service might be a physical plant, such as an adult day center, or it might be a service brought into the home, such as home care.
4. ***Promotion***. This defines how the product will be promoted and how communication will be conducted with potential clients. Promotion includes such items as advertising and purchase incentives. For many LTC services, clients and families are choosing care under pressure, not because it's an elective extra, but because it's a necessity based on an unexpected emergency. This emergency aspect affects the tone and type of promotion.

All of the elements must be in their proper place for the exchange to take place. As an example, the exchanges that take place when a newspaper is sold are relatively simple. A person who wants a paper can choose to have it delivered for a monthly fee or can walk to the corner store daily to purchase the paper. The decision to buy may be based on prior buying habits, advertising, or other incentives, such as coupons included in the paper. The paper must be a good paper that is easy to read (product), be reasonable in cost (price), convenient to acquire (place), and offer some motivation to make the person want to purchase it (promotion).

Applying these principles to long-term care can be somewhat challenging due to the complex nature of the business. A newspaper can easily define its product, its competitive price, the area of distribution, and the promotion needed; the exchange is simple. The exchange is not a complicated one because the person who receives the paper is the consumer.

Contrast this with long-term care services. The client who needs the service may not select the provider organization. It may be selected by the family, recommended by a doctor or hospital, or specified by a health plan. The client may or may not want the service. The client may not even pay for the service if covered by a third-party payer or by family. Additionally, certain restrictions are placed on how the care is provided or carried out. Managed care plans and government programs may place certain limitations on the amount and types of care allowed. In brief, the exchanges that take place in long-term care are many and varied, and the relationship between the client and the service may be much less direct.

How the product or service in long-term care is promoted is also problematic because of the complicated exchanges involved. For a Medicare patient receiving home health, the government may be paying for the majority of the care. However, the initial evaluation of the care will probably be done by the family. Efforts to attract clients may be thwarted because of the lack of contracts, lack of knowledge, or other limitations on the client's choice. The physician making referrals may already know the LTC organization's willingness to provide

The Four P's and Four R's of Marketing	
4 Ps	*4 Rs**
1. Product	1. Recruitment
2. Price	2. Retention
3. Place	3. Referrals
4. Promotion	4. Return

* From A. Sturm. 1998. *The New Rules of Healthcare Marketing.* Chicago: Health Administration Press.

appropriate services and willingness to accept certain types of insurance covering long-term care. Thus the ability to educate the physician about the types of programs offered and the level of quality provided by the LTC organization may be important in developing a strong connection with that physician and his or her referral pattern.

In summary, although the 4 Ps of marketing apply well to many products, they are less appropriate for the healthcare field, and long-term care in particular, due to the complicated nature of the exchanges.

The Four Rs

Sturm (1998) outlines the four Rs of healthcare marketing and accountability, contrasting them to the four Ps (see callout box). Sturm defines the four Rs of healthcare marketing as recruitment, retention, referrals, and return. These are described below:

1. ***Recruitment.*** An organization's goal is to recruit and attract new users; this is particularly true of organizations such as managed care health plans that formally enroll members. Attracting new members from all sources is an important consideration. Recruitment may come from a number of sources: direct approaches to clients, physician referrals,

contracts, and government mandate, among others. For LTC organizations, recruitment is often targeted at families in addition to the direct client user.

2. *Retention*. Retaining clients can be accomplished in a variety of ways, including achieving member satisfaction, family involvement, and contractual compliance. For LTC organizations, retention of clients means providing the right kind of service at the right time in a way that maximizes the client's independence or progress along the continuum of care. Retention also means retaining contracts with managed care organizations and insurance companies, or meeting conditions of participation required to be involved with government programs such as Medicare or Medicaid.

3. *Referrals*. Referrals for LTC organizations come from direct and indirect sources, with heavy dependence on word of mouth. The LTC organization must identify the potential referral sources in its service area and contact those sources through direct selling or indirect public relations approaches. In today's competitive environment, organizations must maintain and expand their referral base. Many organizations have established referral bases that are taken for granted. In the current context of frequently changing contracts, organizations occasionally learn unexpectedly that their organization's previously strong referral base has suddenly contracted with another organization.

4. *Return*. Return on investment has become increasingly important in all of healthcare, including LTC. Assessing market activities for potential return and then actually evaluating the success of the marketing tactic provides useful data for deciding future marketing strategies.

CLIENTS

The organization's clients, as defined for marketing purposes, include all of those parties who have an impact or influence on the decision to buy a product or use a service. Many LTC organizations only view the user of services as the client. Although the service recipient is the end user, many others influence how the service recipient selects the service provider. As noted above, the exchanges involved in healthcare, including long-term care, are highly complex. An organization needs to focus on the correct customer with the appropriate marketing approach. Potential decision makers who become the organization's full complement of clients include the following:

- Service recipient
- Family
- Physician
- Friends
- Hospitals
- Community long-term care organizations
- Government programs (both service providers and payers)
- Health plans
- The community at large

How each client is approached depends on the situation and the understanding of the potential exchange. The benefits—the reasons to conduct the exchange—are quite different for various clients. Physicians make referrals to LTC organizations because they want to help their patients; health plans make contracts with LTC organizations because they want to achieve the most cost-effective use of their funds while meeting contractual obligations to their enrollees. Other decision makers may have their own particular criteria.

RELATIONSHIP TO STRATEGIC PLANNING

Many organizations have two initiatives operating simultaneously, a strategic plan and a marketing plan. The marketing plan should be an outgrowth of the strategic plan; otherwise, resources may be allocated inappropriately. The strategic plan (see Chapter 7) outlines how an organization determines not only what it wants to be and what role it wants to play in the marketplace, but also its core business strategies. The marketing plan should support the core business strategies that evolve from the strategic plan. The marketing plan then requires analysis to ensure that a well-designed marketing plan meets the objectives outlined in the strategic plan.

Market Segmentation

Based on the results of the strategic plan, the LTC organization may want to segment their market and implement a strategy that develops targets within that market. Many LTC organizations will develop a local niche strategy. The niche strategy will concentrate on a particular area or community or service area from which to draw clients, and a particular target sub-population.

Five market segmentation principles should be analyzed when developing a niche strategy. These include that the market is visible or identifiable, available or accessible, amenable to purchase, profitable, and open.

1. *Identifiable*. A sub-market must be identifiable by looking at a geographic service area, target population, and types of potential clients. This also includes potential referral sources, contracts available, and referral networks already in place. The ability to accurately count the clients is one way to determine if the market can be identified with precision.
2. *Accessible*. The market must be accessible and the product that the organization desires to market must be accessible to the client. A new senior housing development on the "new" side of town might represent an unserved market but, realistically, seniors are unlikely to drive across town from older neighborhoods to see it. A satellite office with models might be more appropriate if the LTC organization decides to target this group.

3. *Amenable*. Is the service within the niche market one that clients, families, or payers are inclined to buy? Is the pricing strategy correct? Adult day services have found it challenging to recruit participants even when they are the only local provider and the price is low.
4. *Profitable*. The market niche must be profitable. For example, low-income clients might have limited access to low-cost personal care services. However, if the rates offered by the state's Medicaid, Title XX, or the Older Americans Act programs are all too low to cover costs, home care agencies might target private pay markets instead of low-income clientele.
5. *Open*. The existing market must have sufficient room in it that the LTC organization is able to excel beyond current or potential future competition. This may mean taking a risk and offering a new service before any other organization makes it available, or having a clear competitive advantage: price, a loyal customer base in place, or a cultural or ethnic or religious appeal that will attract clients even if services are identical.

The staff or consultants responsible for the LTC organization's marketing plan should work closely with those engaged in strategic planning to ensure that the products (services) being promoted are the priorities in the organization's plans for its future and that the market niches being targeted are the ones the LTC organization desires to capture. The strategic planning process is also likely to have gathered data that can be useful to marketing in preparing its promotions. By working together, each can help the other, and the result will be a coordinated approach to successful service delivery.

MANAGEMENT AND STAFF INVOLVEMENT

Marketing should be incorporated into management discussions. Marketing should be as important as the budget and should be a regular focus of the executive management team (EMT) or senior management staff. Continued revenues, constant recruitment of new clients and referrals, and community awareness of the organization's attributes are essential to the financial success of the organization.

Managers and employees must be educated about the exchanges and the impact that marketing has on these exchanges. Managers, employees, consultants, and volunteers must all be taught who the target population clients are, what services the clients are seeking, and how to best fulfill their needs. Each potential client has an inherent and unsatisfied need, and the LTC organization has the ability to satisfy that need. How the organization satisfies the need and how it handles communications with this client will greatly determine the success of current and future sales.

TYPES OF PROMOTION

Promotion activities span advertising, personal sales, and public relations. All and any types of media can be used in promotional messages: print, verbal, electronic; mass media or individual. Different methods are effective with different market segments—hence the need to define clearly and understand the exchange preferences of various client segments. Varied activities include the following:

Advertising
- To the general community
- Press releases, human interest stories
- Paid advertisements

Personal Contacts (Sales)
- Personal sales to individuals and/or families
- Personal sales to payers (HMO, PPO, insurance companies)
- Meetings with physicians

- Visits to discharge planners
- Meetings with estate planners, financial and legal counselors

Public Relations and Outreach
- Open houses
- Client activities and events
- Health fairs
- Involvement in local service groups (e.g., Rotary, Lions, etc.)

Electronic Advertising
- Website
- Listserv participation
- Group email constructed with families of clients

ALLOCATING EFFORT

As previously mentioned, the strategic plan will largely determine the direction of the marketing plan. The methods an organization uses to market will depend on its marketing goals, its resources, the market segment targeted, the culture of the community, and the experience and preferences of the staff responsible for marketing.

Whatever techniques are used should be cost-effective and the results measured. The following questions should be asked of each proposed promotion activity:

- Who is the target population?
- Do they make the decision of where they will seek care?
- Are they inclined to make such a decision?
- What outreach approach connects with them: What advertising do they read? What community events do they attend? What sales approach is effective?
- What is the average service use of new clients and the revenue generated?

- How many new clients per year must be admitted just to cover the marketing costs?

Marketing efforts should be market driven and should be evaluated for their cost-effectiveness on an individual basis routinely and collectively at least annually.

SUMMARY

Marketing is the process of creating an effective exchange of goods or services that benefits two parties. For LTC organizations, the exchange is typically for health and related support services. Marketing involves adapting the product, price, distribution methods, and promotion to specific segments of the broader client market. Clients are more than end-users of the organization's services; they include families, friends, physicians, community agencies, payers, and others. A wide array of marketing promotional techniques are available. Those selected by the LTC organization should be evaluated for their cost-effectiveness to ensure appropriate use of scarce resources.

KEYS TO MANAGEMENT SUCCESS

- Coordinate the marketing plan with the strategic plan.
- Know your clients well.
- Establish a structured approach to marketing and follow it.
- Involve all managers, staff, consultants, and volunteers in marketing.
- Select promotional techniques appropriate for each target market.
- Evaluate the cost-effectiveness of promotional initiatives.

REVIEW QUESTIONS

1. What is marketing?
2. What are the 4 Ps of marketing, and how do they apply to long-term care?
3. What are the 4 Rs of marketing, and why are they applicable to healthcare and long-term care?
4. Describe basic promotional techniques. How does an LTC organization decide which to use for a given market segment?
5. What criteria should be used to determine if a proposed new promotion is appropriate for a defined client group?

REFERENCE

Sturm, A. 1998. *The New Rules of Healthcare Marketing*. Chicago: Health Administration Press.

CHAPTER NINE

Licensing, Accreditation, Certification, and Quality

"The time to repair the roof is
when the sun is shining."

John F. Kennedy (1917–1963)

George had been the administrator of a skilled nursing facility for two weeks. He had come from another state and was pleased to have relocated, but the job offer had necessitated that he move immediately, so he had little time to prepare. He was still getting to know the organization and the people, let alone the regulations, the financing, and the community. On Monday morning, the state survey team greeted him when he arrived at 8 a.m. They announced that they were there to do the annual survey. George gulped. He had no idea if the facility was prepared. He didn't know how they had performed on the last survey, or in what areas they were most likely to have difficulties. Being new to the state, he wasn't even sure of the details of the state regs. He had no idea where to find much of the information he'd need, let alone what shape it was in. He did know that the previous administrator had been let go because the facility was having difficulties. George panicked. He blurted out, "You can't come now! I just got here; we're not ready for a survey!" The survey team took out their notepads, jotted down something, and accompanied him into the home.

PROVIDING "QUALITY" CARE is as challenging to long-term care as to other sectors of healthcare—perhaps even more so. Definitions and measures of "quality" care are less developed in LTC at the present time than in acute care. Moreover, quality of life becomes an issue, and quality care provided in someone's home takes on new dimensions than quality care provided in an institution. Select LTC services have long been criticized for their lack of quality, from books such as *Tender Loving Greed* (Mendelson 1974) to formal reports by the Institute of Medicine (Institute of Medicine 2001).

Long-term care organizations span the full breadth of the regulatory spectrum. Nursing facilities are perhaps the most highly regulated of all healthcare services, while private home health agencies and social support programs are among the least regulated of any service providers. Multifaceted long-term care systems span more government and private agencies than the typical acute care system, adding to the complexity of management. Whatever the situation for a specific service, the administrator needs to know the detailed requirements to comply with laws and regulations and to determine the value of accreditation, an external assessment of how the provider is doing. Quality of care should be examined independent of external enforcement and should be an ongoing process pursued by the LTC organization for the purpose of continuously enhancing the efficiency, effectiveness, and sensitivity of care.

Four functions—licensing, certification, accreditation, and quality assurance—collectively represent the organization's commitment to providing quality of care. This chapter discusses each of these four functions.

LICENSING

A *license* is a document issued by a government agency that permits an organization to operate a business. Criteria are delineated by the government unit, and the organization seeking the license must document and/or demonstrate that it meets the specified criteria. Most long-term care services are licensed by the state, although some licenses are issued locally. Table 9.1 shows the government agencies most likely to be responsible for licensing select services.

Table 9.1. Licensing Authorities* for Select LTC Services

Licensing Authority	Service
State department of health services	Hospitals, nursing homes, Medicare-certified home care agencies, hospices, adult day health services (medical model)
State department of social services	Adult day services (social model), residential housing, group homes
State department of mental health	Mental health clinics, group homes for the mentally retarded
State/local housing authority	Assisted living, senior housing, disabled housing (for Life Safety Code compliance)
Business license	Private home care agency, money management services, case management agencies

* Licenses are issued by local government authorities and thus may vary by locality.

Long-term care organizations that are government units may or may not be licensed. For example, a case management company owned and run by individuals may operate under a business license. In contrast, a case management program run by the local Area Agency on Aging, which is a government unit, is not required to have a license.

The license for the organization is distinct from the license for individual practitioners who are employed by or who contract with the organization. For example, an individual physical therapist must have a license to practice from the state agency that licenses health manpower. The free-standing physical therapy clinic at which the therapist works may be licensed by the state under the department of health services as an outpatient clinic. One of the criteria for licensure for the clinic is likely to be that it only employs or contracts with practitioners who have appropriate training and current state licenses.

Licensing criteria typically include the following areas: patient care, patient safety, physical plant, record keeping, fiscal solvency, and staffing. Providers that offer more than one type of service face several licensing authorities, adding to the complexity and cost of compliance. For example, a multilevel complex might have a skilled nursing license from the state department of health and human services, a license from the department of social services for an adult day care program, and a license from the housing authority for a residential care facility.

In some states, some services may obtain a license simply by submitting the appropriate paperwork and fees. In other situations, licensing may be accompanied by a survey, which is an on-site visit by a team of trained surveyors to ensure that the organization meets licensing requirements. The state survey process for nursing facilities is the most infamous. Because surveyors can arrive in teams unexpectedly, the facility must always be prepared. The ideal is to have compliance so ingrained into daily operations that an unannounced survey is not a threat. However, even good facilities have a difficult time keeping up with the ever-changing regulations at federal, state, and local levels. Professional and trade associations and the licensing agencies themselves are the best ongoing sources of information about new regulatory requirements.

Licenses for healthcare service operation are not indefinite; they must be reviewed periodically. A fee is usually charged for initial and subsequent licenses. An organization can also be fined for licensing violations. These fees contribute to the cost of maintaining the licensing and compliance agency.

CERTIFICATION

As used in the healthcare field, *certification* denotes that an organization is authorized to bill the certifying payer. To be certified, an organization must meet the payer's criteria. For example, Medicare certifies select types of healthcare organizations, including hospitals, home health agencies, and hospices. Although almost all hospitals are certified by Medicare, many hospices are not, and there are more home care agencies that are not certified than home care agencies that are.

Certification is neither automatic nor permanent. A provider organization must demonstrate that it continues to meet the payer organization's criteria and must be recertified periodically to maintain its status. The certification criteria established by Medicare and Medicaid are called "Conditions of Participation" (details can be obtained a www.cms.gov/cop). These are articulated in the regulations implementing the original 1965 legislation, along with modifications over the years, and are quite detailed and extensive.

Deemed status applies to the automatic application of certification. For example, many state Medicaid programs accept certification by Medicare as meeting the criteria to be certified as a Medicaid provider as well. This means that the provider organization does not need to undergo a separate survey to document its ability to meet state criteria to participate as a provider in the Medicaid program.

Accreditation agencies may also qualify to award deemed status. A hospital that is accredited by the Joint Commission on Accreditation of Healthcare Organizations (JCAHO) is automatically awarded deemed status by the Medicare program. The result is that institutions must experience only one survey, that of JCAHO. For most long-term care services, deemed status is less available.

ACCREDITATION

Accreditation is evaluation by an external, non-governmental organization, against a set of standards determined by the industry. Accreditation is optional. The benefits to a healthcare organization include the following:

- demonstration of quality to providers;
- demonstration of quality to consumers;
- deemed status (for select services); and

- participation in certain financial programs (e.g., managed care).

The process for accreditation typically consists of preparing specified documentation and undergoing an on-site survey by a team of professional surveyors. The details vary according to the accrediting agency. Table 9.2 lists common accrediting bodies and the LTC services they accredit.

The purpose of accreditation is to ensure quality of care and management—not to penalize willing providers. Thus, most accrediting bodies try diligently to help the agencies they accredit. Accrediting criteria are clearly articulated and publicly available. Accrediting agencies publish documents to help an organization prepare for a survey, and many conduct preparation conferences. Independent consultants are available, and large corporations often have expertise at the corporate level to help their members.

Nonetheless, accreditation can be expensive and time-consuming. Although an on-site survey may only take two to three days, the process of preparing for and following up with recommended changes may take two years. The organization being accredited pays the fee. The organization must review policies and procedures, administrative documentation, and clinical care. Additional work and stress on staff are to be expected. On the other hand, accreditation may offer the organization distinct advantages in attracting clients. Internal revisions may be painful to implement but, over the long run, should benefit the organization in its daily operations. The administrator must weigh the cost and advantages, consider the timing and resources available, and eventually decide whether accreditation is worth the effort and cost.

QUALITY

Until 30 years ago, quality of healthcare in the United States was more or less assumed. Physicians were revered, and hospitals were

Table 9.2. Select Accreditation Agencies and Services Accredited

Accrediting Agency	Services Accredited	Deemed Status
Joint Commission on Accreditation of Healthcare Organizations (JCAHO) www.jcaho.org	Hospitals, nursing homes, home health agencies, hospices, psychiatric hospitals, long-term care hospitals	For hospitals, home health agencies, hospices, for Medicare
Commission on Accreditation of Rehabilitation Facilities (CARF) www.carf.org	Rehabilitation hospitals, comprehensive outpatient rehabilitation facilities (CORFs), adult day services, assisted living facilities	
Community Health Accreditation Program (CHAP) www.chapinc.org	Home care, hospice	Hospice, for Medicare
National Committee for Quality Assurance (NCQA) www.ncqa.org	Managed care organizations	

trusted. Then, challenges arose. Technology provided more data and more tools to examine quality processes and outcomes with objective information. As a result, the healthcare delivery system now confronts the dual challenges of high expectation by clients and practitioners and a wide array of management and clinical monitoring activities, all done in the name of quality.

Quality of healthcare, as is it presently used, connotes a variety of activities and an entire lexicon of terminology. Attaining quality in the delivery of LTC services should be an ongoing process engaged in by an organization because it wants to provide the best care available to its clients, not because it is afraid of a bad report card or a horror story in the newspaper. Moreover, in discussing quality as it pertains to long-term care, quality of life becomes an issue as well.

To date, federal, state, and local governments have taken an approach to quality that is driven by regulatory compliance. For example, nursing homes participating in Medicare and Medicaid are required to have a quality assurance (QA) committee that focuses on four areas:

- Infection control
- Accident prevention
- Monitoring of pharmaceutical practices
- Utilization

LTC facilities must compare their performance to a predetermined standard established by a bureaucratic organization looking for minimal compliance from all facilities. This tends to breed a group of mediocre facilities striving to do no more than comply. Improvement only becomes an issue if the facility falls out of compliance. The system does not encourage continual striving for improvement in all the activities of various departments and activities. For those organizations that genuinely seek to provide quality, a variety of self-monitoring techniques are available.

Continuous quality improvement is a concept of continually examining what an organization is doing and engaging in staff-generated efforts to improve the organization's operations with the goal of improving outcomes. Formal processes have been developed to guide an organization in implementing this type of ongoing analysis/improvement process. These include continuous quality improvement (CQI), total quality management (TQM), and Six Sigma.

Report cards were initiated by the private sector as a way of comparing providers. Recently, the federal government has begun to rate long-term care providers on select measures of quality and to publicize these results. Nursing homes were the first to be examined, beginning in 2002. Nursing facility ratings became available on the website of the Centers for Medicare and Medicaid Services, at www.cms.gov. Similar ratings for home care agencies are also posted by CMS.

Client satisfaction surveys and feedback can provide the LTC organization subjective measures of how clients like the care they are receiving. Feedback on specific activities, staff, and processes can pinpoint areas in which the organization should improve. Positive feedback can be used to praise employees and encourage continued high performance.

Accreditation agencies usually require a *formal quality assurance program*. Those LTC organizations that undergo accreditation will thus establish a quality assurance program, including a team or individual with this designated responsibility, processes for examining quality, and markers or benchmarks for targets.

An LTC organization can address quality proactively, in addition to complying with external demands. The staff and senior managers of the organization can determine areas where they want to excel and set their own performance standards. The managers and staff of the organization then establish their own goals and their own processes for quality achievement.

The Future

In the twenty-first century, healthcare organizations, including long-term care organizations, will have quality improvement as a core business strategy. Administrators will need to establish programs and groups to meet this strategy for long-term success. The strategy will include continuous improvement of the clinical processes as a part of the quality program. This strategy will be in addition to any "monitoring" activities required by state and local reviewers. They will also need to convince reviewers to move to a more process-oriented method of evaluating quality. Additionally, administrators can apply decision theory to quality. Decision theory, as discussed by Griffith (1999), suggests three routes to improving the contribution of medicine to health and affecting clinical quality, as shown below:

1. ***Increasing the value of intervention***
   a. improving the results of therapeutic intervention, improving the outcome for each patient, or increasing the variety of cases for which an intervention is appropriate
   b. improving the discriminatory power of diagnostic tests, that is, the ability to detect whether the patient has a certain disease or condition
2. ***Reducing the cost of intervention***
   a. reducing the danger of harm to the patient
   b. reducing the resources consumed by the intervention
   c. reducing conflict between interventions
   d. reducing the pain or discomfort associated with an intervention
3. ***Reducing the cost of delay***
   a. improving the ability to predict the patient's course, as with an improved diagnostic test or new understanding of the implications of specific signs and symptoms
   b. reducing delays between orders and intervention
   c. reducing intervention failures and repetitions

This approach is clearly much more sophisticated than a mere check-off list approach to compliance.

Managing Quality

Managers must develop a system of quality assurance that will move their organization to higher levels of achievement for clients by incorporating principles of continuous quality improvement with good business practice. Such a system, in addition to meeting requirements from regulatory agencies, needs to emphasize improvement in a special way. It should include the following considerations:

- Improvement efforts can always be improved upon, and attainment of a given level does not mean that the organization can rest.

- Improvement should always be approached from the perspective of the person receiving care: the client.
- Improvement examines all process broadly, including activities not directly concerned but potentially affecting the process.
- Improvement needs to focus on all the steps in the process or the group performance as a whole rather than outliers.
- Improvement programs must be supported by top management, and its commitment must be clear and active.

To accomplish improvement programs LTC managers must gather information that will allow them to implement successful changes. First, such information will need to be able to look at each step in a process and identify unneeded "handoffs" that hinder accountability, where decision points emerge, and the impact from others outside the process. Second, the information will need to be complete so the process can be evaluated for effectiveness. Third, costs and potential problems must be able to be identified readily so necessary adjustments can be identified. Last, one needs to be able to compare the LTC organization's process or steps to other providers to compare steps versus outcomes.

In summary, LTC managers and their executive management teams must develop systems that allow staff to examine critical processes in both client care and administrative areas. For progress to be made there must be willingness to problem solve by looking at organizational processes to improve them and positively impact client care and costs.

SUMMARY

LTC organizations are scrutinized by a variety of external sources. Keeping up with licensing, certification, and accreditation processes is an ongoing challenge. A team approach can help spread the work among senior managers, as well as build widespread commitment throughout the organization. LTC organizations dedicated to quality can also choose to go beyond required activities to engage in ongoing processes to ensure and enhance the quality of care and, ultimately, the quality of life, for their clients.

KEYS TO MANAGEMENT SUCCESS

- Know who licenses the service and verify the date or approximate date of the next survey.
- Get the licensing criteria and make sure the managers and staff understand what they are, how they are interpreted, and what needs to be done to meet them.
- Know who accredits your service. Examine the criteria and resource requirements for certification and determine if it is worth it for the organization to become accredited.
- In conjunction with exploring sources of revenue, know which funding sources require certification or deemed status.
- Allocate the resources—staff time, dollars, expertise—required to ensure success with licensure and accreditation.
- Incorporate quality measurement as a year-round process, not just when a survey team is expected.

REVIEW QUESTIONS

1. What is the purpose of licensure? Who licenses LTC organizations?
2. What does certification mean as applied to the healthcare field?
3. What is *deemed status* and how does it benefit LTC providers?
4. What is accreditation? Name several accrediting organizations and the type of healthcare organizations they accredit.
5. Describe four types of organizational activities that relate to quality of care.

REFERENCES

Griffith, J. 1999. *The Well-Managed Healthcare Organization, 4th Edition*. Chicago: Health Administration Press.

Institute of Medicine. 2001. *Improving the Quality of Long-Term Care*. Washington, DC: National Academy of Sciences.

Mendelson, M. A. 1974. *Tender Loving Greed*. New York: Vintage Books.

CHAPTER TEN

Information Systems

"I think there is a world market for maybe five computers."

Thomas Watson (1874–1956),
Chairman of IBM, 1943

The computer had crashed! The staff of the adult day care center weren't sure who was scheduled to attend that day, what specials services were needed, what diets had to be arranged for lunch, or how they would keep track of the billing. The administrator was out for the day, and no one knew whom to call for help. "Don't we have some old paper files?," asked an aide.

INFORMATION HAS BECOME the driving force of the twenty-first century. We are inundated with information from phones, faxes, computers, televisions, VCRs, DVDs, and cell phones with imbedded digital cameras. Moreover, due primarily to advanced technologies, the expectation is that whatever information one wants should be available almost instantaneously and should be accurate and up-to-the-minute in its currency. The art for LTC organizations is to sift through the myriad of available data sources and techniques to compile the information actually needed to deliver a service efficiently, effectively, and with high quality. By taking a realistic approach to selecting essential technology and training staff in its

---

The first part of this chapter has been adapted from Zawadski and Shugarman, from the second and third editions of *The Continuum of Long-Term Care* by C. Evashwick © 2001 and 2005. Reprinted with permission of Delmar Learning, a division of Thomson Learning: www.thomsonrights.com. Fax (800) 730-2215.

use, the LTC organization can use its resources wisely and not waste scarce resources on extravagant but ineffective technology. This chapter presents a framework for delineating core information, organizing it to be useful, and managing a data system that produces needed management and clinical information on a timely basis.

DEFINITION

An integrated information system (IIS) is an array of multiple information sets linked together in an organized way. Information sets are groups of similar items often collected together. Examples include client characteristics, health and functional assessment, service use, and service billing information. The multiple information sets may be collected at different points in time by different members of the service agency. Instead of collecting information separately for each purpose, an integrated information system links or connects information collected by different units in the agency and makes it available to everyone who needs it. *Organized* means that there is a well-defined plan for collecting and linking information sets to meet multiple information needs in the most efficient and effective manner. An IIS is more efficient because it eliminates the need for duplicate data collection; one entry serves all. Data may be computerized or not. Most importantly, an IIS makes more information available to all users, allowing new and expanded use of information to improve service quality and increase efficiency.

Integration of information can occur at many levels. Within the agency providing a single service, information can be linked across departments, for example, between clinical staff and accounting. Integrating fiscal and client data allows the measurement and tracking of service cost and the assessment of cost-benefit and cost-effectiveness. In the multi-service agency, an IIS would ideally link information across different services and would integrate information across agencies for a single service participant.

Chronically ill persons are not conveniently divided into acute and long-term care segments; their problems and needs are interrelated. Integrating information across services and provider systems provides a comprehensive picture of the participant, description of his or her health needs and conditions, the services received, the cost of care, and the outcomes of treatment. Altogether, this information allows provider-based managers of care to make decisions that improve the quality and limit the total cost of chronic care; in addition, it guides resource allocation decisions and planning for the needs of the client population.

A MODEL INTEGRATED INFORMATION SYSTEM

An information systems model developed by Zawadski to manage an integrated service program for a long-term care population is shown in Figure 10.1 (Zawadski 2001). The boxes identify different sets of information or files. Lines show the connections or links between information sets.

Many pieces of information are needed to manage and deliver high-quality services to a long-term care population in a cost-effective way. These data elements can be grouped in different ways. Multi-service agencies may have several information sets covering the same area; for example, the service recording forms for the daycare center may duplicate those of other departments. In a comprehensive and truly integrated information system, this duplication would be eliminated.

The conceptual model information system is divided into two major areas: the participant and fiscal components. Major information sets in each area are identified and described below. Examples of items included in each set are presented, and data collection source and frequency are discussed.

Figure 10.1. Model Integrated Information System for a Chronic Care Organization

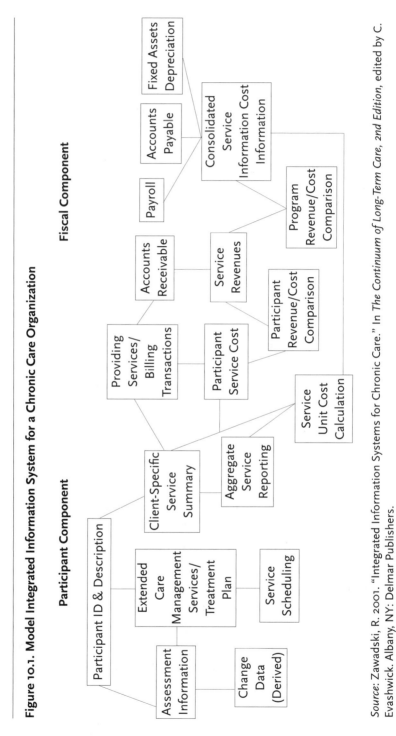

Source: Zawadski, R. 2001. "Integrated Information Systems for Chronic Care." In *The Continuum of Long-Term Care, 2nd Edition,* edited by C. Evashwick. Albany, NY: Delmar Publishers.

Client Information

Identification and Description
Central to an IIS is the basic information identifying and describing the participant. This information is collected at the time of application or enrollment and is used by everyone within the system. The master participant record would include the following fields:

1. Identifying information: name, address, phone, family contact, Medicare, Medicaid, and insurance numbers.
2. Demographic information: gender, ethnicity, date of birth, marital status, and living arrangements.
3. Program status information: eligibility/membership status, application date, referral source, reason for referral, enrollment, and closing date.

   Data collection frequency: This information is relatively stable. Information should be recorded at time of enrollment and updated as changes occur, for example, change of address, or change in program status.

Assessment
Before determining the service needs of a chronic care participant, the person's health and functional status must first be assessed. Assessment information is used to define major health conditions that define service needs. Thus, the assessment should include information on all areas influencing service decision making. Assessments should be repeated at regular intervals to monitor change. Change in health and functional status is an outcome measure. The participant assessment record would include the following items:

1. Health status information: major medical conditions, active medications, review of major health systems, and general health status.

2. Functional status information: level of assistance needed in activities of daily living, and instrumental activities.
3. Cognitive status information: short and long-term memory, reasoning skills, and the ability to make decisions on their own behalf.
4. Environmental information: assessment of living environment for barriers to independence and safety (e.g., stairs, and bathroom facilities).
5. Informal support information: assessment of the informal support (family, friends and neighbors) available, and the assistance they can and do provide.

Data collection frequency: This information changes over time and needs to be assessed at regular intervals (e.g., quarterly or semi-annually). Changes in assessed status will be an outcome measure derived from the comparison of assessments at different times.

Service/Treatment Plan

A service or treatment plan is developed by the care management team based on assessment information. The plan is integrated and cuts across all service areas. The participant and/or family is involved in the development of the plan. The service/treatment plan record would include the following:

1. Service goal information: list of prioritized care management goals developed by the participant and care management team.
2. Service orders: specification of the type and amount of services ordered for the participant (e.g., number of home health visits, frequency of adult day center attendance, scheduled medical procedures, and active meds).

Data collection frequency: This information will be changing constantly as client needs change. An initial plan should be developed at the time of assessment and stored with the assessment record. The service plan record should be continually updated to reflect changes in the plan. The service plan information is used for service scheduling.

Service Use

The service use record tracks all of the health and human services provided to a participant by all service departments or agencies. This information should be collected and organized by service type and amount and is summarized for a given time period. The participant's service record should include these items:

1. Delivered services information: date, provider, type, and amount of health and health-related services provided to the participant by all providers. Services include number of admissions and days of hospitalization, nursing home days, inpatient and outpatient physician visits and procedures, home health and in-home supportive services, durable medical equipment, prescriptions, adult day services, therapy, and medical transportation.
2. Service coordination: date, type, and amount of care management and coordination service provided to the participant by the provider or its affiliated agencies.

Data collection frequency: This information will be collected as individual service records on an ongoing basis. Service information will be summarized and reported for specified time periods (e.g., on a monthly or a quarterly basis). Service patterns can be compared across participants and providers and tracked over time. Service use can also be compared to service plan to assess compliance, one measure of service quality.

Fiscal Information

Service Revenue

Services are paid in many ways (e.g., physicians may be reimbursed per visit or procedure, for hospital stays by DRGs, for adult day centers by day of attendance, and by monthly capitation). One important data set, then, is the amount billed and received for health and health-related services. The service revenue record should include the following elements:

1. Service charge information: the date and amount charged for each health and health-related service provided to participants.
2. Payment information: the amount of payment received for each service from each funding source.
3. For those that participate in health plans, capitation amounts per enrollee.

Data collection frequency: This information is collected, along with individual service records, on an ongoing basis. Total service charge information by participant can be computed on a monthly basis. Revenues for all chronic care services can be reported by funding source.

Service Costs

Charges do not necessarily reflect costs. Where possible, an attempt should be made to capture costs of services. Cost information can be ascertained through the agency's fiscal system or independently gathered from estimates of staff time, facilities, and materials needed to provide the service. A chart of accounts should be established, and expenses should be collected. An expense reporting system can be used to integrate different types of expenses and group them by service area. The program cost record should include the following:

1. Personnel cost information: salaries and benefits for staff involved in the delivery of services by service area; contract prices for professionals engaged on a contract basis.
2. Materials and supplies information: cost of materials and supplies used in the delivery of services. Costs can be grouped by service area.

3. Facility cost information: cost of facilities, use of equipment, and general overhead used in the delivery of services. These costs should also be grouped by service area.

   Data collection frequency: Ideally, this information would be derived from the agency's general ledger system and reported on a regular (e.g., monthly) basis. Otherwise, cost information can be estimated on a periodic basis from multiple sources (e.g., time analysis, or pro-rations of facility use). Total expenditures by cost centers can be compared to service counts for the same time period to measure cost per unit of service. Cost information should be compared to revenue received by service and overall by participant.

Integration Across Multiple Providers

The model described above is a general model for the integration of participant and fiscal data within a single provider organization. The system becomes more complex when attempting to integrate multiple funding streams. The same service may be paid for by more than one payer or program (i.e., both Medicare and Medicaid pay for home health services). The most effective way to reduce duplication of service provision, improve coordination of care across providers and payers, and quite possibly reduce the cost of care is not only to integrate information across different providers within a single organization or program but also to integrate information across providers in different funding streams and over time for the same client.

PRIVACY AND SECURITY

Privacy concerns are raised by integrated information systems. Sharing of data across multiple services and providers will increase the threat to privacy of personal information. The Health Insurance Portability and Accountability Act (HIPAA) is a large and complex piece of legislation passed by Congress in 1996 that included efforts to address potential problems arising from the computerization and standardization of medical records, and other sources of personal health information. Among other provisions, HIPAA called for the development of rules to protect the privacy of health information. The U.S. Department of Health and Human Services was tasked with defining these rules. The new Privacy Rule creates a federal-level floor of protection for health information. The Privacy Rule defines health information, who can access and share it, and under what conditions this information can be shared. The penalties for violating the Privacy Rule can be substantial, leaving many organizations, providers, and state policymakers nervous about developing integrated information systems.

HIPAA also details how the privacy of protected health information should be kept secure. The security of this information— the means by which information remains confidential—is the organization's responsibility. Administrative procedures and physical safeguards (e.g., password-controlled access to data) must be implemented in organizations that deal with protected health information. Protections (e.g., encryption for data transfer) and confidentiality agreements can be built into the IIS to safeguard privacy. However, the threat remains— increased access means greater potential abuse. Increased vigilance will be required and participants may be required to sign releases of information. The benefits of IIS for the participant should outweigh the costs and justify these risks. The costs of improving system security are considerable but security enhancements to information systems are required by law and should not be used as an excuse to not develop integrated information systems.

MANAGEMENT'S ROLE

Senior managers of LTC organizations do not need to be experts in data or computers to take advantage of the sophisticated information systems that are available. Senior managers do need to be knowledgeable about the uses of information and be able to manage and guide this function, as follows:

1. *Determine what information is needed.* The key contribution of senior managers to an organization's information system is defining what information is needed and for what purposes, and then analyzing and reviewing the specified information once it is made available.

2. *Assign responsibility.* Someone in the organization should be responsible for information systems. This person should suggest ways to make information more accessible, improve data collection and transfer, recommend new software or hardware, determine vendor selection and evaluation criteria, etc. Although senior managers must ultimately make decisions about these issues, developing at least one internal staff member with information technology expertise can assist and facilitate management decision making. In organizations where no staff member is already knowledgeable, identifying a potential information expert and sending the person for training may be necessary for the organization to develop that internal expertise.

3. *Establish an information technology committee.* Such a committee should include the perspectives of staff who deal with clinical, financial, and client-related issues. Although a single person may have the responsibility for technical knowledge about information systems, an information technology committee can be useful to bring in complementary views on what information is important to gather, how data can be used, and barriers to data collection and use.

4. *Formulate an information technology plan.* This should outline the organization's software and hardware needs for the present and projected two to three years into the future. The plan should have a cost-benefit analysis for each application. Significant effort must be invested in the security and back-up

systems so that vital information is not lost or compromised. Documentation of software and hardware should be maintained and be readily accessible for seeking emergency assistance. Future needs, once identified, should be budgeted in operating or capital budgets.

5. ***Motivate staff to use information technology.*** Training is the most effective way to achieve use. Senior managers should encourage employees to use data produced by the information systems to improve efficiency and quality.

VENDORS

The potential use of external contractors relates to many different departments within the LTC organization, including information systems. An outside service will often have resources and expertise that a small LTC organization does not have. Outside contractors are available for information systems and provide the following services, among others:

- System design
- Software (package or custom) and software support
- Hardware and hardware support
- Consultation
- Financing

External experts may be particularly helpful in the developmental stages of information systems. A consultant can be helpful in evaluating the existing information, identifying what additional data are needed, and developing strategies for accomplishing information objectives. Many vendors are available. Selecting one that is good, and that will meet your needs, train your staff, be available when you have an emergency, and still be in business when you are ready for your next upgrade—these are the important criteria beyond the immediate contents of the system.

SUMMARY

Quality of care, cost efficiency, and accurate reporting are forefront issues in all aspects of healthcare, including long-term care. Increased oversight by public agencies, competition among providers, and ethical scrutiny related to accurate records are all bearing down on healthcare organizations. As a result, the health and human services sector is finally joining other industries in realizing the importance of IIS in accessing data records and providing quality products. Recently enacted government regulation is aiding the move to integrated systems by requiring the computerization of patient/client information. All of this means that healthcare organizations must equip themselves with IIS to maximize quality, manage costs, and meet external reporting demands from both payers and consumers. Accomplishing this in long-term care is particularly challenging due to the use of multiple services by clients, both simultaneously and sequentially; the varied information systems required by the federal government for different long-term care services; the low operating margins of most long-term care entities; and the extensive use of staff with minimum education. These challenges make the manager's role in implementing an effective information system all the more important and call for a proactive stance by management in embracing the use of sophisticated information technology of the future.

KEYS TO MANAGEMENT SUCCESS

- Appoint or recruit a strong manager to be responsible for information technology.
- Establish a multidisciplinary committee to review information technology operations on an ongoing basis and evaluate new requests for software, hardware, or information collection.
- Develop a plan to improve data collection and the information technology functions on a continuous basis; accommodate the plan in the organization's budget.

- Develop electronic systems for clients and families to access information about the LTC organization.
- Anticipate requirements of payment programs and be proactive in developing information systems that access the needed data easily.
- Encourage and reward staff for appropriate use of advanced information technology. Include education about computer use in in-service and continuing education programs for staff.
- Understand the capabilities of the information systems to maintain a good balance between clinical, fiscal, and administrative applications.

REVIEW QUESTIONS

1. What are the main components of the ideal integrated information system?
2. What privacy considerations of HIPAA influence today's information systems?
3. What criteria should be used in selecting vendors?
4. What actions should a senior manager take to guide the information systems function of the organization?

REFERENCES

Shugarman, L., and R. Zawadski. 2005. "Integrated Information Systems." In *The Continuum of Long-Term Care, 3rd Edition*, edited by C. Evashwick. Albany, NY: Delmar Publishers.

Zawadski, R. 2001. "Integrated Information Systems for Chronic Care." In *The Continuum of Long-Term Care, 2nd Edition*, edited by C. Evashwick. Albany, NY: Delmar Publishers.

CHAPTER ELEVEN

Space and Equipment

"A doctor can bury his mistakes but an architect
can only advise his clients to plant vines."

Frank Lloyd Wright (1868–1959)

*Zoey Jones, case manager for Community Services, was trying to fig-
ure out how best to help her 77-year-old client. Mrs. Zapeta had
slipped on the front stairs of her home during the cold, icy winter. She
had broken her hip and had been in a hospital, skilled nursing facility, and rehabilitation hospital during the recovery process. Now she
was mobile with a walker and ready to be discharged. However, her
home still had five stairs up to the entrance, and inside the house, the
bedroom and the full bathroom were on the second floor. Clinically,
Mrs. Zapeta was ready to be discharged, so Zoey didn't expect that the
insurance company would let her stay longer at the rehab hospital or
even a skilled nursing facility. If her house had a different arrangement,
she would be fine to go home with home care. Under the circumstances,
going home wasn't a practical solution.*

*While Zoey pondered this dilemma, she battled frustrations with
her own space. Her office was small to begin with, and she shared it
with another case manager. Although they weren't always in at the same
time, when they were, they had to take turns making phone calls,
because two people talking at the same time was too confusing. This
space problem delayed task completion. Moreover, her computer was
old and slow and frequently crashed, so going online to explore available, affordable assisted living facilities wasn't practical. A new system
was supposedly coming soon, but budget cuts had forced a delay. She*

just wanted to slip away to a quiet place to get a cup of coffee and review Mrs. Zapeta's file without her phone ringing. However, the staff coffee room was used for meetings when the conference room was in use, and right now, the room was occupied.

PEOPLE, MONEY, REGULATIONS, and *space*—these are the functions that take a manager's time. Space has several facets: design, construction, capital finance, equipment and furnishing, and placement of people. The environment, including physical space, affects how a person can function and, conversely, how a person functions affects the type of environment in which they can thrive. The environment thus affects client care, staff productivity, and morale. For staff, space can be a highly charged issue. Space is a critical tool that a manager must master to accomplish other management responsibilities. The purpose of this chapter is to raise awareness of the impact of space and equipment on the LTC organization's operations.

PHYSICAL ENVIRONMENT

The physical environment affects both staff and clients. Many managers take space for granted. They do not think about how space can be changed to the benefit of clients, staff, and management. Managers planning new LTC facilities can have a major role in creating internal and external layout. Even when the physical plant layout is fixed, numerous interior elements can be altered.

Staff

LTC is a difficult business to work in emotionally and often physically as well. The physical environment needs to be as conducive as possible to facilitating client care and preserving staff energy. Many clients are unable to perform ADLs, and staff are often taxed physically to assist in transferring, walking, bathing, and other tasks. The layout of the physical plant should be as convenient as possible; for example, resident functions should be placed adjacent to one another to minimize the distance required for residents and the staff assisting them to walk under pressure, like when trying to get to meals on time.

Staff should also have a quiet refuge to go where they can escape the immediate demands of clients and families, recover from an emotionally difficult encounter with a family or client, and recoup their own physical and mental health.

Assigning staff offices is a challenge faced by managers. Care must be taken to facilitate respective work tasks of individual staff. When offices are shared, of course, personal needs, preferences, and personalities should be considered whenever possible. Careful consideration of initial office assignments is important. If it becomes necessary later to move a staff person from one office to another, work is disrupted and tempers may flare.

Long-term care is unusual among businesses in that staff and volunteers may well perform their duties in a client's home; for example, home care agencies send out personal caregivers to homes, and volunteers deliver Meals on Wheels. Staff working in a home are exempt from standard office monitoring, a situation that can cause problems if a client accuses a staff member of inappropriate behavior. Also, useful equipment might not be readily available or obstacles to care might be present. Thus, those who will be working in someone's home must be trained about how to function in someone's home as a place of work. Performance evaluations must also be revised to apply to work done independently and in varying settings.

Clients

Most people prefer to remain in their own homes, even when they are frail and unable to function independently. Thus, modifying the client's home environment to allow them to remain at home becomes a high priority. The LTC professional must be able to assess a client's home and make realistic recommendations about changes in the physical environment that will facilitate independence. Many modifications can be made at very low cost but can make a very large difference in safety or functional ability; grab bars can be added in tubs; door handles can be changed from knobs to levers, and lights can be put on timers.

Formal instruments for home assessment are readily available. Occupational therapists typically perform such assessments, but others working in a client's home can be trained to identify space issues, either formally or informally. Staff sensitivity to environmental issues should be incorporated into staff in-service education, whether the staff goes into a person's home in the community or into a room within an LTC facility.

Visitability and *universal design* are two concepts currently popular with architects and interior design experts. Visitability refers to enabling someone who has a disability, such as a wheelchair user, to visit a home comfortably. Examples of high-visitability features include lack of steps to enter the house, absence of high doorframes, and a wheelchair-accessible bathroom on the main floor. Universal design refers to a comprehensive approach to designing new construction that incorporates into the original construction many features that will enable a person with functional disabilities to adapt his or her home to future needs. Advocates of these types of physical plant requirements for institutional settings, as well as private homes, are now promoting public policies pertaining to construction that will cause new buildings, whether commercial or residential, to be built with universal design features from the beginning. The Center for Housing Modification (www.homemods.org), is an excellent resource for information on home renovation and physical plant design.

DECOR AND AMBIANCE

In recent decades, knowledge has increased greatly about how the design and decor of the physical environment affect a person's behavior and performance. The field of long-term care is particularly sensitive to how the physical environment affects an individual's ability to function independently. A manager in an LTC organization should periodically evaluate the work environment from the perspective of both clients and staff. Features to look for include those that affect physical performance and those that affect mood or behavior.

General features examined should include lighting, signage, color scheme, floor covering, entrances and exits, and odor. Details that influence functioning and therefore should be assessed include types of door handles, ease of opening doors, convenience of pull-cords, size of clock numbers, and hearing-enhancement buttons on phones.

Experts in physical design for specific LTC populations are somewhat rare but can be found, perhaps through a university gerontology program, and invited to do a site evaluation. Occupational therapists can be helpful in identifying hazards and potential remedies. Just following a staff member or a client around for an hour a day over the course of a week is one way to observe physical barriers or facilitators and has the added benefit of demonstrating concern and compassion.

For clients with dementia, the design of the physical space can provide many clues that facilitate functioning. Nameplates on doors of assisted living facilities or SNFs help residents return to the correct room, as does using color-coded paint or rugs to help residents find their way. A collage of pictures from earlier years helps residents reminisce, and a glass shadow-box for family memorabilia outside rooms can assist residents in identifying their personal space. It also personalizes space and stimulates conversation among residents. Hanging clothes in order in the closet helps those with poor vision select clothes that match.

The Eden Alternative (www.edenalt.com) is an approach to the environment of residential care facilities first proposed by Dr. William Thomas. Dr. Thomas asserts that bringing in life to the residential care facility improves the mood and well-being of residents, as well as the staff. According to Dr. Thomas, the Eden Alternative "is founded on the idea that the physical and social environments in which we deliver long-term care can and should be warm, smart, and green" (Thomas 2003). Examples of how LTC organizations can be modified include growing plants inside and outside in client-controlled gardens using waist-height planter boxes that do not require stooping or bending, bringing in pets like dogs and cats, having aviaries and fish tanks, and otherwise making the environment feel very much alive.

The Eden Alternative approach combines enhancement of the physical environment with resident activity, for the betterment of both. For example, in one senior housing complex, a rose garden became the specialty of one of the residents who had always had a hobby of horticulture. He brought two dozen specialty rose plants when he moved in. He remained physically more active because of his gardening, the women residents loved getting fresh roses from the garden for their rooms, and the facility had a beautiful walking garden open to residents and families, at minimal cost to the facility. Pet therapy is another formal approach to creating an environment for residents that radiates warmth and caring.

In summary, the way the environment is decorated and arranged can help minimize frustration and maximize independent functioning of clients and also contributes to a more harmonious work environment for staff. The physical environment can help create a positive ambiance for care and human interaction.

EQUIPMENT AND FURNITURE

The science of ergonomics has become increasingly sophisticated during the past 50 years. How equipment is designed and placed can maximize or handicap the performance of a staff member or client. This is particularly the case for people with functional disabilities.

Some managers might take the position that replacing equipment or furniture that is poorly designed is too expensive. However, the cost of one worker's compensation claim or one lawsuit from an injured client can far exceed the costs of proper equipment. Moreover, any organization, no matter how small its margins, should establish a depreciation account or donation allocation to plan for replacement.

Managers can take a proactive role in determining how appropriate the existing equipment and furniture are. Surveys of clients and staff, focus groups, complaint boxes, and monitoring of worker's comp claims or client injury reports are all routine ways of gathering consumers' input. Watching ads in trade magazines and reading articles on new technological advances are other ways to identify opportunities for valuable upgrades or modifications. When the strategic plan of one older facility resulted in a recommendation to change the target audience, the facility conducted focus groups of community members and current residents to find out what interior design elements appealed to the new target audience, including types of chairs and couches, style of decoration, and color schemes. Renovation was planned and funded anyway, so letting the "new" target audience participate in the design helped market the new service direction, as well as ensure that the facility would appeal to the desired new clients.

New equipment and furniture should thus always be a planned future occurrence. Even if it's a five-year time frame, at least employees and clients will know improvement is coming. The knowledge that management is sensitive to staff and clients' needs will, in and of itself, have a positive morale value.

LTC organizations, like all other organizations, are constantly confronted with changing computer operations, both in software and hardware, and other new medical technology and its accompanying equipment. The costs of the computer software and hardware and new technological equipment should be included in the annual budget. In addition, training for staff and access to help are two essential features that make new equipment more useable. Many staff of LTC organizations do not have extensive experience in using computers, and many medical devices are brand-new technologies with which no one is familiar. Management needs to overcome fear and ineptitude by letting employees know that they do not expect immediate knowledge of new technology and that they are willing to train employees in the use of new technology, whether software or hardware. Time and resources must be allocated for these functions. An ongoing contract for assistance or support should be included with the purchase of new equipment or software.

Managers can minimize the frustrations and anger caused by computer or technology glitches if they establish an atmosphere that accepts the challenges that occur with technology upgrading as inevitable and work with staff to ease their learning curve rather than blaming them for delays or errors of usage.

REGULATIONS

Several sets of federal laws govern space, and all LTC organizations must comply with these to a greater or lesser degree.

The Americans with Disability Act (ADA), passed in 1990, had the overall purpose of preventing discrimination on the basis of disability. Provisions of this law require physical plants to be accessible to persons with disabilities. The standards are quite detailed and include requirements for exterior physical plant, interior plant, and equipment. Elements cover a wide range, such as drinking fountains and passenger loading zones. These standards must be followed in planning, building, or renovating. Two documents detail the code: the American National Standard Accessible and Usable Buildings and Facilities (Building Officials and Code Administrators International 1992) and the ADA Accessibility Guidelines for Facilities (U.S. Department of Justice 1991).

The Life Safety Code applies to hospitals and federally qualified nursing facilities, among other healthcare institutions. This code was written and is maintained by the National Fire Protection Association, a private, nonprofit organization. It is not a government agency, nor does it write government regulations. One of its volunteer committees, the Committee on Safety to Life, established the

Life Safety Code in 1913 and updates it every three years. When Medicare was first passed into law, participating facilities were required to comply with this code as a way of protecting the safety of the residents and staff. The Life Safety Code focuses first on safety, but it covers a wide range of exterior and interior physical plant elements: physical design, room furnishings, doors, ramps, smoke detection systems, emergency egress, lighting, and so forth. Detailed requirements are delineated in the periodically updated *Life Safety Code Handbook* (National Fire Protection Association 2003).

The Occupational Safety and Health Act (OSHA) was passed in 1970 to promote safety in the workplace. Employers are required to provide a workplace environment free from recognized hazards that could cause harm, or even death, to employees. It is administered by two federal agencies, the National Institute of Occupational Safety and Health (NIOSH) and the Occupational Safety and Health Administration (OSHA) in the Department of Labor. Standards that LTC organizations are required to comply with include the Life Safety Code, mentioned above; the Standards for the Physically Handicapped (American National Standards Institute 1980); and volumes of additional standards. Inspections and reporting of accidents are also components of the required compliance. More information can be found from OSHA or NIOSH or their state counterparts.

FINANCING

Raising the capital, or large sums of money, required for physical plant construction or renovation is a major challenge, no matter how much or how little is required. Chapter 6, "Financing," discusses sources of capital for new construction and major renovation. *Depreciation*, in accounting terminology, is a budgeted line item of funds specifically designated for the replacement of routine wear and tear on equipment and buildings. Managers should set aside funds for depreciation as a regular part of each year's budget. The senior management team might decide how best to spend these funds, or they might ask for staff or client input.

Fundraising is the source of capital for many organizations, particularly those that are nonprofit and that have a loyal constituency in the community. Donations for capital are often easier for individuals and corporations to make because their contribution yields visible evidence: a wing of a building, a piece of equipment, a new van, any of which might carry the name of the donor. Even family members may be persuaded to donate small equipment and furniture that increase client comfort or independence.

Community outreach and fund-raising should be ongoing efforts of every service, whether for-profit, nonprofit, or government. Bringing the community in helps the LTC organization keep its physical space in top shape—we all clean up before we hold a party at home. Even a home care agency whose staff do most of their work in the field spruces up for an annual open house or "bring your kids to work" week. Bringing in visitors lays the foundation for asking for contributions—or even ideas—to improve space.

SUMMARY

The environment can have a major impact on clients and staff. Managers should actively and regularly evaluate the impact on staff and clients of physical space, including layout, interior and exterior decor, furniture, and equipment. Depreciation for routine upgrades and capital finance for major changes should be incorporated into the LTC organization's financial planning.

KEYS TO MANAGEMENT SUCCESS

- Analyze the positive and negative effects of current space and equipment on clients and staff.
- Train staff to be aware of the environment's effect on clients.

- Learn and comply with federal, state, and local regulations pertaining to the physical environment.
- Continuously seek client and staff input about the physical environment.
- Plan for and budget depreciation to fund continuous renovation and replacement.
- In equipment purchases, include resources for maintenance assistance and staff training.
- Build reserves or exercise capital financing for major capital expenditures.
- Establish a fund-raising program, however modest, devoted to environmental improvements.
- Change the environment to be consistent with changes in services, clients, and staff.

REVIEW QUESTIONS

1. Give two examples of how space affects a client's functional ability.
2. Give two examples of how space and equipment affect staff's ability to perform their tasks.
3. What is the Eden Alternative?
4. What two elements should be added to the cost of purchasing new high-tech equipment (e.g., computers or medical devices)?
5. Name and explain three sets of regulations that govern an LTC organization's physical space.
6. What is depreciation? How is it relevant to the physical plant quality?

REFERENCES

American National Standards Institute. 1980. *Standards for the Physically Handicapped*. Washington, DC: American National Standards Institute.

Building Officials and Code Administrators International. 1992. *American National Standard Accessible and Usable Building and Facilities* (CABo/ANSI A117.1). Country Club Hills, IL: Building Officials and Code Administrators International.

National Fire Protection Association. 2003. *Life Safety Code Handbook, 6th Edition*. Quincy, MA: National Fire Protection Association.

Thomas, W. 2003. "Eden Alternative." http://www .edenalt.com/welcome.htm, March 4.

U.S. Department of Justice. 1991. *Americans with Disabilities Act of 1990. Accessibility Guidelines for Facilities. Federal Register* Vol. 56, No 144, Friday, July 26, 1991. Final Rule Part III CFR 28, Part 36.

CHAPTER TWELVE

Ethics

"It has become appallingly obvious that our
technology has exceeded our humanity."

Albert Einstein (1874–1955)

Despite having dementia, Mrs. Jones wandered around happily. She seemed to enjoy interacting with the staff and participating, to the extent she was capable, in a variety of activities. She also enjoyed eating. Her family was very concerned that she was gaining too much weight, and this would be bad for her heart condition. Their position was that Mrs. Jones did not understand the potential negative consequences of her actions, and it should be the staff's responsibility to monitor her eating and not allow her to eat indiscriminately. Whenever they came to visit, they would chide the staff. The senior management team discussed this problem and what policies and procedures it suggested. Although seemingly a simple issue, how Mrs. Jones' situation was handled represented the organization's stance on patient's rights, family rights, patient competence, staff responsibility—in short, a swirl of complicated ethical issues.

ETHICS HAS BECOME a personal and public issue for all managers throughout all industries, including healthcare. The healthcare industry has traditionally been a staunch supporter and believer in integrity, professional conduct, and ethical behavior, because of its mission of care for the sick and needy. However, as payment, length of stay, and access to care issues increasingly affect healthcare facilities, managers are faced with a variety of serious ethical issues on a daily basis.

Long-term care treatment is influenced by ethical issues that derive from client and family interaction, provider behavior, culture and religion, as well as delivery system structure and financing. Ethics in long-term care is a greater challenge than acute care in many instances due to the long duration or permanence of the illness and the functional disability of the client.

This chapter provides an overview of the ethical issues that face the long-term care administrator from organizational, clinical, and managerial perspectives. The ethics of the leader and the ethical values of the organization for which he or she works should be the framework from which ethical decisions flow. However, the long-term care manager is also affected by the many regulations, laws, and policies governing the care of the long-term care client.

ETHICS IN BUSINESS

Business ethics and corporate compliance responsibility programs facilitate the long-term care organization's reaction to both internal and external forces that may challenge ethical behavior. Following a professional code of ethics (such as that of the ACHE or ACHCA) and adopting a personal code of ethics is required in today's environment and is one of the techniques that a long-term care manager can use to guide decisions posed by ethical dilemmas.

On a day-to-day basis, the long-term care manager will face ethical issues that challenge his or her inner strength. Some of these are listed below:

- Client access to long-term care
- Rationing of services
- End-of-life treatment
- Patient/client autonomy
- Application of competency guidelines in the organization

- Policy on futile care
- Confidentiality of records
- Client abuse
- Patient restraint issues
- Framing of management and organizational ethical issues
- Finance ethics

Access

Access to healthcare is one of the overriding issues currently faced by the nation. More than 40 million people lack basic health insurance. This problem is greatly magnified for long-term care. Fewer than nine million people have long-term care insurance, leaving the major sources of financial access as private pay or Medicaid. The LTC senior managers must be concerned about client access to their services. A balance must be achieved between a person's ability to pay and sufficient revenue for the LTC organization to remain financially viable.

Access raises important questions for most administrators. Is it ethically wrong to deny clients access to our services? Should all clients have access to our services? What happens when a client runs out of money? Is care discontinued? These questions must be reviewed and determined as a matter of policy. The LTC organization's policies should be consistent with its resources and mission. Policies should be clearly written and communicated accurately to clients as well as staff. Knowing the policies in advance of a crisis makes it easier for staff to make decisions and to act consistently over time and with many clients.

Scarce Resources

The optimal use of scarce resources poses a challenge for all healthcare organizations, including those in LTC. This issue juxtaposes what is good for an individual against what is good for society; in academic terms, individual justice versus social justice. Questions that arise include the following:

- How far do we go in treating clients? Do we provide clients with every treatment possible or do we resort to rationing services based on the client's level of reimbursement?
- What is our ethical obligation to a client whose reimbursement will not be sufficient to cover needed services?
- Do we ration services or cut back on services when faced with potential financial crises in the LTC organization? Is the greater good to maintain a reasonably strong financial picture and to remain in business while at the same time reducing the level of services to clients?
- How do you determine what an adequate level of service is at a time when long-term care organizations are cutting costs?

These are very difficult management problems that the LTC manager must face. It is best to anticipate such problems and develop a policy that has been reviewed by the board before a concrete situation arises. One way to do this is to use the community standard of care and compare the organization's policies to other long-term care organizations and programs. If the community standard is to transfer or discontinue service when clients cannot pay, does that fit with the mission and vision of the LTC organization?

Nonprofit religious organizations and for-profit proprietary organizations may take very different approaches because their goals and financial situations vary. As long as policies are clearly stated and communicated, clients, families, and staff know what to expect and what factors may affect care planning.

Client Autonomy

Autonomy is the right of the individual to make decisions for oneself. In general, it should be considered at two levels. The first is how

Types of Autonomy

Direct versus delegated autonomy refers to decisions and actions made by the individual versus the delegation of those decisions and activities to another person.

Competent versus incapacitated autonomy focuses on the decisional capacity of the individual making decisions.

Authentic versus inauthentic autonomy moves beyond competency to examine whether the choice is in keeping with the individual's personal history and values.

Immediate versus long-term autonomy recognizes that choices made now may interfere with autonomous action in the future.

Negative versus a positive right. As a negative right, autonomy demands freedom from interference; as a positive right, support and enhancement of choice are required.

Source: Curry, L., and T. Wetle. 2001. "Ethical Principles." In *The Continuum of Long-Term Care, 2nd Edition*, edited by C. Evashwick. Albany, NY: Delmar Publishers.

the agency or decisional autonomy is treated (i.e., how the individual is empowered to exercise autonomy). The second action is the extent to which the person has freedom to carry out the course of action chosen, which may be facilitated or inhibited by the organization. The accompanying callout box shows types of autonomy.

The Patient's Self-Determination Act (PSDA) was implemented in late 1991. This federal law requires healthcare facilities such as hospitals, nursing homes, and home care agencies to inform clients at the time of admission of their rights to participate in healthcare decisions and to execute advance directives, such as living wills, or to designate a surrogate decision maker or healthcare agent. The law also requires facilities to have policies that allow individuals to exercise their rights and to document in the medical record whether the individual has a formal advanced directive.

All LTC organizations should have a formal position regarding client self-determination and client rights. The organization must balance the need for standardized processes with the need for client choice. From a client dignity standpoint, programs should allow client choice and allow a level of client autonomy.

The most frequent ethical question that occurs in long-term care is, "Who makes the decision regarding care?" The competent client is allowed to make his or her medical decisions regarding the kind of care to be received, within payment parameters. A competent client may have the ability to make the decision, but not get the service because of the level of reimbursement for services that he or she may request or demand. For those who cannot make decisions, the LTC management and staff must have ways to determine how such decisions should be made appropriately and legally.

The most systematic and easy method is that of the advanced directive. These are directives formulated by individuals while competent and declare preferences regarding future treatment. These directives may be informal letters or statements that provide an indication of client wishes or formal living wills and durable power of healthcare attorneys.

What happens, however, when there is no "document" to use in making care decisions? In this situation, the physician, clinical professional, and LTC manager must often rely on reports from family, friends, or other caregivers regarding past statements or behaviors that would indicate the client's wishes.

The term *substituted judgment* refers to situations in which the decision maker, with regard to care for the client, uses knowledge of the client's preferences and actions prior to incapacitation to make the decisions the person would have made were he or she still competent. In most cases, the standard used will be what is in the best interest of the client, balancing the expected burdens and benefits to the client.

The "best interest" standard, however, might be overridden by the client's expressed desires. When these issues become cloudy because of a lack of advanced directives, most organizations will rely on discussions with the family, clergy, and friends. Many times, they will also appeal to an ethics committee (discussed later in the chapter) for further advice.

Client Competence

As noted above, implementing the goal of client autonomy is affected by the client competence. Client competence is an initial and ongoing concern for most LTC organizations. Each organization must specify how it will determine competence, what measurements or tools will be used, how often or under what circumstances the assessment will be applied, and finally if the client is determined not to be independently competent, who will be allowed to make decisions on his or her behalf.

The first question is primarily a legal question. The determination of competency is usually made by a court, and the basis for making that decision rests on information provided to the court regarding the client. Each state or county establishes its own criteria.

Many times, the difficulty implementing competency in a LTC setting has to do with the concept of rationality. Competency for the long-term care organization is the question of whether the client is competent to make a decision, not whether he or she is making a rational decision.

Competent clients may refuse further life sustaining treatment. Some may believe that this is not rational. The client who competently decides to forego dialysis treatments, realizing that this decision will end his or her life, is nonetheless competent but, to many, is making an irrational decision.

When clients are admitted to LTC services, every effort should be made to obtain information about preferences for care. Medicare-certified providers and many other LTC organizations require that new clients be asked about completing an advanced directive. This presents the opportunity to discuss preferences and to put a record on file. As a matter of policy, then, it helps clarify any issues of client preferences that may come to pass in the future.

If an incompetent client is admitted for care by an LTC organization, steps should be taken to ensure that decisions are made appropriately and consistent with the client's wishes. A written policy might be developed that outlines the step the admissions staff and clinical staff should use in determining the client wishes, in consultation with family and others involved. If family are available, the LTC organization should endeavor to agree with them ahead of time about what this client would likely direct to be done if he or she were competent. Establishing care parameters with the family in advance saves the LTC staff ethical dilemmas later, as well as potentially saving the LTC organization from lawsuits.

Futile Care

Issues of futile care will continue to grow as medical advances and technology push the age expectancy further. LTC providers may reach a point where care is no longer helpful or beneficial to the client. How is this handled, especially if the family is unsure about what to do? Just prolonging life with no benefit is of no value to the client. A policy defining guidelines for futile care should be developed and approved for use in such situations. For example, should a skilled nursing facility continue to provide nutrition and hydration to a resident who is in a persistently vegetative state? The facility's policy should be clear in this regard and define under what circumstances nutrition and hydration are considered to be extraordinary means. Having explicit policies helps staff, as well as families, know what actions are appropriate.

When such a policy is implemented, staff and physicians must be educated about how to use the guidelines. Ongoing education is essential for new staff and for reinforcement. Having an ethics committee where people can come and express their points of view and get issues resolved helps foster communication and deliberation, and this can be built into the policy.

Issues of futile care often become very emotional. The LTC manager can be most effective if guidelines have been developed for use in determining a course of action. Many times, the clergy for the family and friends must be involved to resolve the action. Whenever families are facing death, family history and behavior patterns tend to resurface, and one must be sensitive to these issues. The LTC organization can assist clinical professionals to perform their responsibilities by having a mechanism in place so that these family issues can be resolved in the best interests of the client.

Patient Confidentiality

The individual's right to confidentiality and privacy is among other ethical and legal issues made more complex across the continuum of care. Ideally, records of medical and other issues should be passed on to caregivers as the client moves through the continuum. Clinical information shared across providers enhances quality of care. Financial information is necessary to determine eligibility and payer parameters affecting care. However, sharing information has been complicated by increasing public concern regarding privacy of health information and access to medical records.

HIPAA, the Health Insurance Portability and Accountability Act, was a landmark legislation in this regard. Healthcare professionals and staff should be aware of the legal requirements, as well as their ethical duties, to protect confidentially and fully inform clients about information-sharing requirements.

LTC managers must know how the provisions of HIPAA affect their organization. Policies need to be formulated and communicated to staff. Additionally, clients must be informed about how such client information will be used and not used. Most organizations now require that clients fill out forms indicating their awareness and acceptance of the organization's policy about how client information is going to be used. This is done upon admission and documented in the client's file.

ETHICS COMMITTEES

LTC organizations have found that forming an ethics committee is a helpful way to deal with the variety of ethical issues that arise. The principle roles of the ethics committee are to (1) formulate policy, (2) educate staff and other professional providers who work with the LTC organization, and (3) offer recommendations when called upon for a consultation for a specific case. The American Association of Homes and Services for the Aging notes that ethics committees are on the rise (www.aahsa.org).

The consultative role of the ethics committee is to advise physicians, staff, and family facing a difficult ethical issue who need help in clarifying the issues. Clients, physicians, or staff might bring difficult situations or problems to the committee for advice. The emphasis is on advice, because it is ultimately the physician or the family that must make the decision, not the ethics committee.

Through policy development, ethics committees properly formed should be able to address a number of key issues that are likely to be faced by the organization. Once these policies are developed, then education and communication with the staff and clients and families should occur on an ongoing basis. The ethics committee should also be responsible for keeping the policies up to date.

Ethics committees should be multidisciplinary and represent a broad range of perspectives. Members are typically physicians, nurses, social workers, clergy, and administration. Some may be consultants or on contract rather than full-time employees. An expert ethicist, if such a person is available, can be an invaluable committee member. Some LTC organizations also invite consumers to participate. Topics about which the ethics committees can develop policies and provide education include the following:

- Advanced directives and the Patient Self-Determination Act
- Decision-making guidelines for an incompetent patient without an advance directive
- Decision making by the competent patient
- Futile care guidelines
- Employment issues including:
  - providing references
  - employee confidentiality of records
  - employee access to records
  - employee layoffs
  - employee discipline and termination
- Conflict of interest guidelines
- Gift acceptance guidelines

The ethics committee can and should be a vibrant, active group, working on existing policies, but also looking proactively to define new ethical issues that may become problems for the LTC organization in the future. By anticipating such problems, developing a policy and related procedures, and educating the staff and clinical providers, difficult situations can often be avoided.

MANAGEMENT ETHICS

Ethical issues faced by LTC organizations are far more than just clinical or client issues; management issues exist as well. Senior managers of the LTC organization play a vital role in setting up the mechanics for ethical issues to be solved and in modeling ethical behavior.

Two professional organizations of healthcare managers have well-written codes of ethics. The American College of Health Care Administrators (ACHCA) is a professional organization of long-term care administrators. ACHCA has developed a code of ethics that revolves around four expectations for the long-term care administrator. These expectations are summarized in the accompanying callout box, "ACHCA: A Summary of the Code of Ethics."

American College of Health Care Administrators
A Summary of the Code of Ethics

Expectation One: Individuals shall hold paramount the value of persons for whom care is provided by providing high-quality care, operating the facility consistent with laws and regulations, developing policies that are consistent with professional standards including protection of confidentiality of the individual, performing administrative duties with personal integerity, and taking steps to avoid discrimination.

Expectation Two: Individuals shall maintain high standards of professional competence. The long-term care administrator will acquire and maintain competencies necessary to perform their duties and actively strive to enhance knowledge and expertise in long-term care. Administrators must be willing to seek appropriate counsel from others when necessary.

Expectation Three: Individuals shall strive in all matters relating to their professional functions to maintain a professional posture that places paramount the interest of the LTC organization and the residents. The long-term care administrator will avoid partisanship and provide methods for fair resolution of any dispute that might arise in terms of service delivery. Likewise, the administrator will disclose to the governing body or other authorities any potential personal conflict of interest.

Expectation Four: Individuals shall honor their responsibilities to the public, their profession, and their relationships with colleagues and members of related professions. The healthcare administrator shall foster increased knowledge within the organization and support research efforts toward this end. The administrator will participate with the community in a plan to provide a full-range of services, share his or her expertise with others increase awareness, and inform the ACHCA Standards and Ethics Committee of actual or potential violation of this code.

Based on www.achca.org. Used with permission.

The American College of Healthcare Executives (ACHE) has also developed a code of ethics. As a condition of membership, a healthcare executive agrees to abide by this *Code of Ethics* and apply it in daily professional activities. The ACHE code of ethics (see www.ache.org) covers five broad areas:

- The healthcare executive's responsibilities to the profession of healthcare management
- The healthcare executive's responsibility to patients and others served, including the organization and employees
- Conflicts of interest
- Healthcare's responsibility to community and society
- The healthcare executive's responsibility to report violations of the *Code*

This *Code of Ethics* is a very comprehensive document and can be a guide for healthcare managers working in any setting, including long-term care. Additionally, ACHE has developed separate ethical policy statements on the following topics:

- Healthcare information confidentiality
- Ethical decision making for healthcare executives
- Creating an ethical environment for employees
- Handling impaired healthcare executives
- Ethical policies regarding decisions near the end of life
- Ethical issues related to a reduction in force
- Ethical issues related to staff shortages

With the support of the ethical statements from these two professional associations, LTC managers can proactively develop policies and educational presentations for their staff and contract providers. Other management and clinical issues that require careful consideration, and possibly institutional policies, include:

- The long-term care organization's responsibility to the community
- How advertising is used to market the LTC organization
- Managed care ethics
- Merger or takeover management
- Use of client or employee information
- Ethics in the following employment practices:
  - Sexual harassment
  - Hiring practices
  - Employee termination procedures
- Implementation of institutional advanced directive policy
- Ensuring compliance with advance directives
- Dealing with noncompliant clients
- Downsizing
- Conflicts of interest
- Impaired executives, physicians, or other professionals
- Financial management

EVALUATION

An LTC organization can evaluate how it addresses ethnical challenges using several approaches.

Conduct an ethics review. This will determine if any ethical issues have been brought to the attention of the senior clinical staff or administrative staff. If no issues have been brought to attention in the past year, this could be an indication that the ethics education program is lacking in some way.

Formally survey employees, physicians, contract providers, senior managers, and governing board members. This can be done by mail or via the telephone with a structured instrument. The survey should ask what kind of ethical issues the organization has faced and if these were resolved to satisfaction. Recommendations for the future should also be solicited. Staff at all levels in all departments should feel comfortable voicing concern, whether by survey or personal meeting, about ethical issues without fear of reprisal from the organization. Such issues may deal with treatment of staff as well as care of clients.

Assess managers' ethical behavior. Managers must abide by the same ethical principles that they advocate for staff. ACHE publishes an annual ethics self-assessment questionnaire for healthcare executives that can be found at http://www.ache.org/newclub/career/ethself.cfm.

Review the activities of the ethics committee. Questions to evaluate the ethics committee include the following:

1. Does the committee have structure? Does it have a purpose and a mission? How frequently does it meet?
2. What is the composition and competencies of members? Do members include clinical staff and members of the clergy? Are arrangements in place with an ethicist who can be called in difficult situations?
3. Does the committee itself engage in policy recommendations and education?
4. Does the committee have organizational and leadership support? Is the chairperson an important leader (formal or informal) in the organization?
5. Is an expert involved who is actively engaging and teaching the members of the ethics committee about relevant topics, including ethics theory, recent bioethical issues, business and managed care issues, relevant health law and other professional and ethical codes of conduct?

If ethical issues are surfacing in the LTC organization, if these issues are being examined by the executive management team or ethics committee, and if the organization is actively educating and promulgating recommended policies and procedures, the LTC organization can feel confident that it has a vital ethics program.

ULTIMATE RESPONSIBILITY

LTC organizations are faced with two conflicting and competing interests. One is the need to provide quality care; the other, to be cost-effective. At times, these two conflict, creating difficulties for managers and staff alike. Ultimately, management must set the standards and implement the procedures for making decisions. Many of the ethical issues that LTC managers deal with require decisions to be made on a personal basis. For many situations, no single decision may be correct. To guide administrators in a very practical way, CEO Austin Ross, FACHE, (Ross 1992) offers the following:

> When resolving ethical questions, you may not always know whether the decision you are making is the right one. There may come a point at which you cannot afford to deliberate any further, and you must make a decision and hope you can live with it. The questions listed below were designed by Laura Nash (1989) to assist with ethical decision making. Your responses may help you to clarify your reasons for making the decision you made. If you feel comfortable with your answers, you have probably made the best decision you can make under the circumstances.
>
> 1. Have you defined the problem accurately?
> 2. How would you define the problem if you stood on the other side of the fence?
> 3. How did this situation occur in the first place?
> 4. To whom and to what do you give your loyalty as a person and as a member of the corporation?
> 5. What is your intention in making this decision?
> 6. How does this intention compare with the probable results?
> 7. Whom could your decision or action injure?
> 8. Can you discuss the decision with the affected parties before-making the decision?
> 9. Are you confident that your decision will be as valid over a long period of time as it seems now?

10. Could you discuss without qualm your decision or action to your boss, your CEO, the board of directors, your family, and society as a whole?
11. What is the symbolic potential of your action if understood? If misundersood?
12. Under what condition woud you allow exceptions to your stand?

If a manager can answer all of these questions to his or her personal satisfaction, the manager can feel that he or she has made the best decision possible under the circumstances.

SUMMARY

Autonomy, the right of an individual to make decisions for oneself, is a fundamental ethical premise to consider in service delivery. Special familial rights and societal norms may affect individual autonomy. External system influences affect the individual's autonomy as well. Older people and those with disabilities are at increased ethical risk for a number of reasons, including ageism, physical and cognitive impairments, and fragmentation of services.

Effective attention to ethical issues requires proactive consideration and planning. Structures and formal mechanisms support health professionals to address ethical dilemmas they face in providing care across the continuum. Carefully thought-through policies and procedures that are well-documented and disseminated are crucial. The organization of an ethics committee for purposes of education, promulgation of policies and procedures, and review of difficult cases has proven effective for many LTC organizations. In-service and continuing education for staff, physicians, and contract providers alike can help ensure uniformity in application of the organization's ethics procedures.

LTC managers must lead by example, demonstrating ethical decision making with regard to the organization's actions and their own personal actions. Professional associations have developed codes of ethics that identify core ethical principles and guide decision making. The codes of ethics of the American College of Healthcare Executives and the American College of Health Care Administrators are most applicable to long-term care managers.

KEYS TO MANAGEMENT SUCCESS

- Learn about basic ethics principles and their applicability in long-term care.
- Find or develop a code of ethics to guide personal and organizational behavior.
- Develop an interdisciplinary ethics committee for the organization.
- Engage in ongoing education about ethics issues, for individual managers as well as all of those who interact with the organization as staff, contract providers, physicians, or family members.
- Conduct annual (or more frequent) reviews of ethical practice behaviors for yourself and the organization.

REVIEW QUESTIONS

1. List and describe four generic ethical challenges an LTC administrator is likely to encounter in daily operations.
2. What is the Patient Self-Determination Act and why is it relevant to LTC providers?
3. What are the three roles of an ethics committee?
4. What techniques can an LTC administrator use to ensure that his or her own behavior is ethical?
5. Who is the ultimate decision maker with regard to ethical issues of client care?

REFERENCES

American College of Health Care Administrators. 2004. *Code of Ethics.* www.achca.org.

American College of Healthcare Executives. 2004. *Code of Ethics.* www.ache.org.

Nash, L. 1989. *Managing the Moral Corporation*, 245. Boston: Harvard Business Review.

Ross, A. 1992. *Cornerstones of Leadership for Health Services Executives.* Chicago: Health Administration Press.

PART III

Managing Your Future

CHAPTER THIRTEEN

Moving From Management
to Leadership

*"Obstacles are those frightful things you see
when you take your eyes off your goal."*

Henry Ford (1863–1947)

PREPARING FOR THE future and evolving into a leader are goals
that many managers desire, but many postpone seeking because of
the pressing demands of each day. An immediate crisis or a problem to solve always seem to distract managers from assessing how
their leadership will shape the future of the organization. Just as
strategic planning is imperative for the organization, evolving from
managers to leaders is essential for those responsible for the future
of the long-term care organization. Chapter 1 differentiated the
skills and traits of managers from leaders. This chapter further
examines the leadership competencies needed for the future,
describes the necessary relationship skills, including emotional intelligence, and identifies executive styles that contribute to the effectiveness of professional leaders.

CORE COMPETENCIES NEEDED BY
LEADERS OF THE FUTURE

Earlier chapters address the core functions that senior managers
must master through academic training and experience. While

knowledge of these functions is important, it is not sufficient to distinguish a competent manager from a leader. Kruger-Wilson and Porter-O'Grady (1999) identify core competencies needed by leaders in the healthcare organizations of the future. They include four broad areas:

1. *Leadership Competencies.* Leaders must possess strong business skills, including technical expertise in organizational design, financial management, economics, business ethics, evaluation methodology, information technology, and LTC strategic planning. Increasingly, the business world, including healthcare, is one of managed interdependence. Relationships with other organizations are increasingly important as organizations become increasingly interdependent.

2. *Conceptual Competencies.* Leaders must apply conceptual skills using inquiry and critical thinking. Leaders understand the primacy and value of the whole and the relationships that exist among the parts. Managers must learn to live in chaos but also recognize how the organization interacts with other organizations. Executives must engage in continuous learning to keep a broad perspective on day-to-day problems and future trends.

3. *Participation Competencies.* Leaders must become skilled at generating full involvement of others. Leaders foster opportunities for shared decision making and collaborative projects and encourage input from others while emphasizing the value of staff contributions. They create an environment in which staff understand that shared decision making is preferable to individual decision making. Articulating and publicizing the benefits of high participant involvement are a key part of all communications.

4. *Interpersonal Competencies.* Leaders must act as facilitators and be effective communicators. Communication can no longer be dominated by task-oriented or authoritarian messages; leaders encourage democratic communication. Leaders

must also become skillful in group and team dynamics, learning to guide staff performance through counseling and mentoring. They must solve performance problems while maintaining positive relationships. Leaders also must communicate shared meanings across multiple constituencies.

The first of these broad areas, called leadership competencies, reflects the management functions described in preceding chapters. A core body of knowledge and application tools for these competencies can be learned, either through academic study or on-the-job training. A competent leader in LTC must have basic knowledge of these skills but can hire specialized staff to handle technical functions, such as accounting, on a daily basis.

However, the remaining three competencies involve interaction with others in communications and work assignments. These skills can indeed be learned, not only by reading a book but through sensitivity and practice. They are particularly important for the leader of a long-term care organization due to its focus on providing care to people, depending on people to produce the primary product, and connecting with other organizations to receive and make referrals, providing clients with a comprehensive continuum of care. The following section elaborates on these essential relationship skills.

RELATIONSHIP SKILLS

Leaders of the future must value the contribution of other partners. According to Kruger-Wilson and Porter-O'Grady (1999) this requires several concrete relationship skills:

- Partnering skills
- Team-building skills
- Work-organizing skills
- Mentoring skills
- Emotional intelligence

Partnering Skills

The most sought-after skill in executive management of LTC facilities is the ability to partner with others, an ability that is key to the success of the LTC organization. LTC organizations have numerous organizational exchanges, many partners, and many different clients. The ability to see the points of view of others and relate these to the objectives of the LTC organization is essential. Identifying a partner's objectives and aligning these with the objectives of the LTC organization can create a shared vision, which is a critical goal. The needed partnering skills include an assessment of one's ability to work with others, the ability to listen to another's point of view, the ability to bring parties together for discussion, and the skills to conduct meetings so that people of diverse orientations leave with positive feelings and a common goal.

Team-Building Skills

Effective managers and leaders must develop team-building skills, including how to select the right team members, how to facilitate meetings, and how to create award-winning teams. Recent management literature extols the use of teams, recognizing the potential power that a correctly selected team can bring to the organization (see Chapter 5). Objectives are not achieved by one or two individuals alone; service is provided along the continuum of care and reflects the collective efforts of many. Thus, the development and effective use of teams are essential elements to the effectiveness of the LTC organization of the future.

In developing teams, the manager needs to ensure that teams are cross-functional and multidisciplinary. Team members must also be able to transcend the perspectives of their particular role or discipline and to consider the productivity of the team as a whole. Over time, such teams can become highly effective, reflecting a broad management approach and expanding staff capabilities. Sometimes an external facilitator can facilitate the team-building process, although the leader may also serve as the facilitator. Regardless of who serves as facilitator, the support and encouragement of top leadership is always a critical element in team building.

Work-Organizing Skills

In today's LTC organizations, leaders need to reassess how work is organized, distributed, and accomplished. Perpetuating traditional work methods in the cost-reduction environment of today puts pressure on the caregiver and frustrates the client. Leaders must challenge traditional assumptions about how work is organized. Multiskill training of staff and assessing the degree of control leaders exercise are just two of many issues to be addressed. The ability to identify potential partners within the continuum of care is also necessary.

Mentoring Skills

LTC executives also need to develop the ability to mentor the professionals who work with them, especially management professionals. A true leader seeks to build leadership among others, and this fosters a commitment to the job and to the organization. Once a person has committed to his or her job and to the organization, behavior changes. For example, expected behavioral changes might include the following:

- Staff have control over their work and make judgments about client care and client flow along the continuum.
- Staff use self-scheduling systems to review their own schedules and make adjustments.
- Strong management staff members avoid directing but instead coordinate, facilitate, and remove barriers so that workers can act more productively.

As skilled workers become knowledgeable workers, staff will increase their ability to improve client care. The ability to manage along the continuum, rather than provide a specific set of services, will greatly determine how LTC organizations will succeed in the future.

Emotional Intelligence

Emotional intelligence is another important skill-set that is crucial to leaders and to the success of their organizations. Emotional intelligence, as defined by Dye (2000), involves energy and maturity. Energy is sometimes defined as the spark or zeal for life, and refers to the liveliness with which leaders approach their work and which contributes to their stamina.

Maturity, on the other hand, refers to refinement, social graces, tact, the ability to grow and change, and the ability to correctly interpret signals from others. Maturity enables us to empathize, to have a sense of humor, and to respect others. It enables us to express gratitude, to harbor no ill will, and, when wrong, to apologize. Although emotional maturity is often associated with older executives, it also can be learned at a young age.

The emotionally intelligent leader is a more effective leader, one who relies on staff to assist the organization to achieve goals. Such a leader also has a high degree of respect for the contributions of employees in improving the organization. Five dimensions of emotional intelligence involved in effective leadership are described below:

1. *Self-awareness* involves continual self-assessment by the executive and a realistic sense of one's own strengths and weaknesses, coupled with a strong confidence in one's own abilities.
2. *Self-regulation* is the sense of integrity that the executive possesses in choosing the ethical response. Developing feedback mechanisms, understanding one's own intentions, and taking

time for self-reflection of a critical nature will help the leader improve his level of emotional intelligence.

3. *Motivation* characterizes responsive leaders. The leader's enthusiasm and level of motivation will be reflected in how the organization accepts challenges.

4. *Empathy* is needed to understand the emotional and motivational make-up of others. The ability to relate to difficulties, aspirations, goals, and family issues assists leaders in leading others more effectively.

5. *Social skills* are needed to assist effective leaders. Social skills enable the leader to be directly involved in each relationship and each conversation. Social skills are necessary to the leader's ability to influence, collaborate, and cooperate, not only within teams and within the organization, but also outside the organization as well.

Each of the above five dimensions is an essential component of emotional intelligence. The effective leader will periodically assess the extent to which he or she has developed these dimensions, will seek evaluative input from others, and will seek opportunities to develop further along each of these dimensions.

EXECUTIVE STYLE

In addition to the qualities addressed above, an effective leader will also become cognizant of his or her own leadership style. While basic personality remains stable over time, behavior can indeed be changed, and leadership behavior can be learned. The organizational literature often addresses elements of leadership style. Griffith and White (2002) identify six aspects of executive style that are important for strong leaders: predictability, candor, responsiveness, persuasiveness, conflict resolution, and participation. Each of these is defined below.

1. *Predictability*—A leader that handles similar situations in similar ways and follows predictable cycles of behavior creates less stress on the organization and its members.
2. *Candor*—Candor in communication helps employees understand how the organization is operating and the challenges and opportunities it faces.
3. *Responsiveness*—Management is responsible for responding to the questions and concerns of staff, clients, and others. The leader's responsiveness improves the morale and stability of an organization's workforce.
4. *Persuasiveness*—Effective leaders have a superb ability to speak in front of groups, to articulate a position, to mesh current activities in the marketplace with current activities of the organization and to evolve plans for the future.
5. *Conflict Resolution*—Quickly resolving the inevitable conflicts provides predictability. Skill in conflict resolution engenders confidence in the organization's ability to solve problems, remove disruptive barriers, and focus the group on common goals.
6. *Participation*—As a general rule, organizations that solicit input and involve staff and clients are more likely to succeed than those that rely only on input from a few.

Self-realization is the beginning of self-improvement. A leader who seeks to improve his or her own effectiveness can assess his or her management style and skills using any of the many tools or programs available through professional associations, universities, or other training organizations.

SUMMARY

In LTC organizations, the charge is to care for clients compassionately and effectively. The manager's ability to stand up for his or her own values and ethics will communicate to clients that the organization is a safe and caring place to be. Many of the skills that leaders need to develop relate more to the artful skills of management as opposed to technical knowledge. As previous chapters noted, partnering with others, seeing others' points of view, and remaining strong in the face of adversity are all abilities requiring the qualities addressed in this chapter.

Effective leaders will learn from their mistakes. Effective leaders understand their staff and develop compassion for them as well as for clients. Leadership is important to the success of the organization, and staff attribute traits of knowledge, ability, competence, and intelligence to positions of leadership. Leaders need to earn this recognition from staff by continually developing their own abilities.

Leaders also need to examine their ability to manage the dynamics of many varied relationships. An executive's ability to manage relationships will be the key differentiator in the marketplace of the future. Not finance, not just clinical skills, not legal knowledge, but relationship abilities will be the abilities sought by employers.

The management of people is not a science; it is an art. It is an art such as playing a guitar, an art that is developed over time, with experience and practice. Leadership is also an art that requires continual review, occasionally requires a change of strategies, and, above all, requires honesty with self.

KEYS TO CAREER SUCCESS

- Assess your management skills and style.
- List the qualities you would like to see in your supervisor and emulate them.
- Seek feedback on your ability to relate to individuals and groups of people.
- Evaluate your typical reactions to stressful situations and consider alternatives.
- Engage in continuing education on a continuous basis.

REVIEW QUESTIONS

1. What are the four core components of leadership identified as important by Kruger-Wilson and Porter-O'Grady?
2. What are the essential relationship skills identified by Kruger-Wilson and Porter-O'Grady?
3. What is emotional intelligence and why is it important in today's work environment?
4. According to Griffith, what are key critical aspects of executive style?
5. What can a manager do to become a leader?

REFERENCES

Dye, C. 2000. *Leadership in Healthcare: Values at the Top.* Chicago: Health Administration Press.

Griffith, J., and K. White. 2002. *The Well-Managed Healthcare Organization, 5th Edition.* Chicago: Health Administration Press.

Kruger-Wilson, C., and T. Porter-O'Grady. 1999. *Leading the Revolution in Healthcare, 2nd Edition.* Gaithersburg, MD: Aspen Publishers.

CHAPTER FOURTEEN

Managing Your Career

"If a man insisted on being serious, and never
allowed himself a bit of fun and relaxation, he would go
mad or become unstable without knowing it."

Herodotus (484 BCE – 430 BCE)

WHETHER LEADER, MANAGER, senior staff, or new junior staff, each individual is ultimately responsible for managing his or her own career. LTC may be the field explicitly chosen, perhaps due to fondness for one's grandparents or a bonding with a friend with a disability. Or, it could simply be where one arrived fortuitously, perhaps through a college internship or a summer job. Regardless of how one entered the field of long-term care, to succeed personally and professionally requires managing one's career as well as one's job. Personality and the unexpected events of life affect everyone. Nonetheless, definitive actions for career success are within the control of each professional. This chapter outlines strategies recommended for personal career management.

DETERMINE WHERE YOU WANT TO BE

For most people in the Western world, the early part of life is governed by a time frame of three-to-five-year blocks: society conventions more or less govern when to start kindergarten, finish elementary school, go through junior high, complete high school, and proceed through college. Each of these experiences has a fixed time, clear goals, and a predetermined next step. Many people also know in advance the specific educational institution at which they will take each step. After one graduates from college (or high school) and enters the world of full-time work, goals and time frames and next steps are absent and the location and institution of one's daily job uncertain. Many people never take control of their lives or careers after early childhood education.

Those in long-term care have many career options. As noted in Chapter 2, the types of long-term care organizations number more than 60, and the nation has more than 60,000 long-term care businesses. Each person seeking a career in LTC needs to find his or her niche. The people who succeed in long-term care do so because they love their work: they are particularly good at working with people and are highly sensitive and sympathetic to the human condition. Once a person realizes that he or she is comfortable with long-term care and that he or she wants to stay in the field, job opportunities are extensive, and climbing to the top quickly is a realistic goal.

Those whose careers appear to run the smoothest are the individuals who identify the type of position they want, the type of LTC organization in which they wish to work, and what they want to be doing in three to five years. Just as the organization must set goals and measurable objectives, so should individuals, particularly those who have the clear desire to climb the ranks to become senior managers and leaders.

Some may be fortunate enough to identify their ideal future job early in their work experience. For others, searching may be necessary. Talking with others in the field about what they do can help distinguish types of LTC roles. Students may arrange times to shadow LTC executives or staff. Visiting colleagues at their place of work can differentiate types of organizations. Attending meetings of trade or professional associations is a good way to gain exposure to many senior managers. Executive search firms and outplacement firms may have knowledge of jobs that are less common. Whatever approach is taken, the LTC manager needs to have a general answer to the question, "What do I want to be doing three to five years from now?"

ESTABLISH A PLAN

Just as organizations need strategic plans, an individual needs a career plan. A three-to-five-year time frame is most realistic, although a longer-term goal may underlie short-term activities. A personal plan should parallel the organization's plan in having one or more goals and shorter-term, measurable objectives. Once a career goal has been identified, the LTC manager should delineate the skills, experience, education, and relationships that will be needed to be eligible for the desired position. The next step then becomes determining what is needed to achieve maximum capability in each of these areas.

For example, if a person's goal is to become the administrator of a skilled nursing facility, a license from the state is needed. This entails identifying the criteria that qualify one to take the exam and getting on course to meet these requirements. This may mean spending time as an administrator in training or taking academic training at a certified university. It may also involve preparing for the exam, studying, taking a weekend blitz course, forming a study group with others preparing for the exam, or similar concrete tasks. Meanwhile, a second goal might be to obtain a job in a corporation that owns SNFs to be positioned to become an administrator once licensed.

A third related goal might be to achieve senior status in the professional association for nursing home administrators, the American College of Health Care Administrators (ACHCA), or the broader healthcare managers' association, the American College of Healthcare Executives (ACHE). Achieving fellowship status in either is a multi-year process, involving participating in continuing education programs, taking an exam, and writing fellowship papers.

Three-to-five-year future plans are useful for professionals at every stage of their career. Although the oft-spoken phrase, "life is what happens while you are planning," may indeed be true, those who have a plan for their career are much more effective in making career-related choices that keep them moving in the direction toward where they want to be in the long run. Even those who are approaching the end of their career need to have retirement plans in place to make this transition smooth for the organization, the individual, and the individual's family.

So, setting up a folder for one's personal career goals and a time each year to review it, be it in January in conjunction with making New Year's resolutions or in June in conjunction with preparing a June 30th fiscal year-end report, can be a highly structured but very useful way to evaluate where you are, where you are going, if you are making timely progress in the right direction, and additional steps you can take to advance your goals.

KNOW YOURSELF

One aspect of envisioning your future and preparing to get there is knowing your strengths and weaknesses. Leadership can be learned and exercised by people of all personality types. However, it does help managers to know their own styles and how they interact with people—particularly in long-term care, which is a people business.

Formal tests are available to help managers understand their personality, management style, and communication effectiveness. Self-assessments are common; however, techniques are also available to enable a manager to obtain the opinions of others. For example, performance appraisals done of the LTC manager by his or her boss can be used in a positive way as a diagnostic tool. An assessment by the people who interact with the manager at all levels, called a 360-degree assessment, is another technique. Pursuing external testing takes time and resources, but informal evaluation by friends and peers may be done easily and at no cost.

Making an honest list of "things I like to do" and "things I don't like to do" is another simple way of sorting through career choices to rule out positions that just aren't a good fit. Articulating personal preference parameters further focuses career choices: family considerations, geographic preferences, and desired salary and salary limits, among others.

PREPARE FOR CONTINUOUS LEARNING

College students often have the illusion that once they pass the last course, they'll never need to take another test or pull another all-nighter. In today's rapidly changing world, any healthcare professional, whether in clinical care or management, must be prepared for continuous learning. Technology and knowledge are changing so quickly that a professional must be active in seeking continuing education to stay current.

Education can be gained through formal programs offered by trade associations, professional associations, universities, or proprietary training companies. The means can range from attending a seminar to reading a book to asking a knowledgeable colleague for a hands-on training session. Those fortunate enough to have had a mentor should put the effort into maintaining this relationship; those without mentors should seek to find a mentor or close colleague, even in mid-career. Distance learning has become popular as a way to access experts without the necessity of leaving one's office.

Whatever the method used, a manager should set aside the time and allocate the resources each year to acquire a designated amount of education. The topic should be selected to further one's job or career goals. Those who must meet requirements for continuing education credits, such as nursing home administrators and clinicians like nurses, have an external force providing carrots or

sticks for ongoing education. Those who don't have such requirements should take it upon themselves to design and adhere to a personal educational program.

BUILD RELATIONSHIPS

Professional relationships are extremely important for those working in long-term care. Such relationships come into play for business
reasons, like seeking and making referrals, and for personal reasons,
like looking for a new job or finding emotional comfort after the
passing of a special client.

In large organizations, peer groups may be found internally.
However, many LTC organizations have small management staffs.
Establishing relationships with peers can be a challenge, as it involves
going outside of one's day-to-day sphere of activities.

Involvement with entities other than one's employer takes extra
time, but in return, provides opportunities to take leadership roles
in preparation for assuming a leadership role within the LTC organization.

Professional and trade associations are, once again, obvious
choices. Membership is usually related to job or institution. Most
professional associations charge fees. A few require members to document their credentials as a prerequisite for joining. Professional and
trade associations typically have large annual meetings in a central-
ized location but smaller meetings throughout the year that are
designed for local areas. They present access to education, as noted
above, as well as opportunities for networking. Leadership opportunities arise in serving on or chairing committees, helping plan the
annual meeting, and submitting abstracts to present papers or otherwise participate as faculty in seminars put on by the association.
Many communities have informal groups of LTC professionals who
meet on a regular basis, monthly or quarterly. These are often con-
vened by the Area Agency on Aging or a local healthcare delivery
system. Other local opportunities for establishing relationships with

businesses come through groups such as Kiwanis, Rotary, or the Chamber of Commerce. Being on the board of a local organization is another way to meet like-minded people and gain experience beyond one's immediate LTC organization. Many nonprofit organizations seek out civic-minded people for voluntary boards, so willingness to participate may be the only criteria sought.

Networking is an art, and one that should be learned and practiced. Always carry business cards. Set goals for the minimum number of networking meetings to attend each year or quarter. Have at least one lunch per month with someone you don't know well or haven't seen in a while. Keep a rolodex, even if it's an email address book. Have a party occasionally to invite people to your LTC organization or home. Relationships can be built and maintained in many ways. They don't come automatically, so this takes work. But, in the long-run, a little effort toward building relationships produces a large return for one's business and career, as well as providing support and often enhancing one's satisfaction with career choices.

EDUCATE OTHERS AND GIVE BACK

Once a manager has established a secure position or advanced to a leadership role, giving back to the community through education accomplishes several purposes, including building relationships, giving visibility to the LTC organization and the individual, and learning through the process of teaching others.

Educating others can take the form of mentoring a single individual (such as taking an administrator in training at a nursing facility), taking an intern (such as a student from a local university), guest lecturing, teaching a full course, writing a paper for a professional journal, or developing a relationship with a university for research and demonstration projects. Few universities have programs specifically focused on long-term care management. Most, however, have courses on general management, gerontology, or human development. Universities with clinical health professions training programs may have specialties in geriatrics or may be delighted to have interaction with a health-related organization of any type.

Other ways of giving back to the community include donating to local charities, sponsoring community activities (such as children's sports teams), volunteering for boards, or making the LTC organization's common areas available to community groups for select meeting times. These goodwill gestures improve one's self-esteem as well as personal visibility in the community.

STRIVE FOR BALANCE

All individuals should strive for balance in life. Senior managers and leaders, especially in today's chaotic healthcare field, run the risk of being so absorbed with their business obligations that they neglect their own career and their family. Too little sleep, too much stress, too many long days detract from, rather than enhance, a manager's work performance and, ultimately, job satisfaction. The manager's energy level and enthusiasm on the job have a direct effect on the efforts of many others, clients as well as staff and colleagues. Managers thus need to structure their schedules to allow adequate personal time for their family and for themselves.

ENJOY YOUR JOB

Ideally, every person should enjoy his or her job. People work harder and are more productive when they enjoy what they are doing. LTC is a very challenging field. The demands placed on managers are extreme at times, and the rewards can be high in emotional satisfaction but sparse in wages or amenities. Overall, one should be glad to go to work every morning and, at the end of the day, believe that the day's work has made a positive contribution to people's lives. A manager in LTC who truly does not enjoy his or her job will not have the patience, the enthusiasm, or the drive to handle the many management challenges that arise. Knowing when to move on is important.

Despite its challenges, LTC has many positive aspects: human warmth, kind people, and heartfelt stories. Being able to appreciate these elements is essential to the ultimate success of the manager of an LTC organization.

SUMMARY

Careers must be managed, just as organizations must be. The manager of an LTC organization must have a plan for his or her own future, similar to the strategic plan for the organization. Elements should include position aspirations, needed skills, formal education, and financial targets. Networking on a regular basis helps to develop a base of colleague support that can help when the manager needs information, support, guidance, or the next position. Lifelong learning is essential in today's world, where information and the environment are changing so rapidly. Balance in personal and professional time and enjoyment of one's position are essential to long-term retention and success in any position.

KEYS TO CAREER SUCCESS

- Develop a three-to-five-year plan for what you want to be doing and how to get there.
- Monitor your progress and revise your plan on an annual basis.
- Know yourself; engage in assessments of your management style and skills.
- Participate in life-long learning.
- Balance family and personal needs with job demands.
- Enjoy your job!

REVIEW QUESTIONS

1. What techniques can be used to learn more about the types of roles available in LTC?
2. What elements should be included in a personal career plan?
3. What techniques can help a manager assess his or her own personal style?
4. Identify several methods for continuing life-long learning.
5. Why is building relationships important to your career plan? Identify several ways to build relationships.
6. Why is balancing your career with your personal life so important?

Suggested Readings

Bennis, W., G. Spreitzer, and T. G. Cummings (editors). 2001. *The Future of Leadership*. San Francisco: Jossey-Bass.

Berkowitz, E. 1996. *Essentials of Health Care Marketing*. Gaithersburg, MD: Aspen Publishers.

Certo, S. C. 2000. *Supervision: Concepts and Skill Building, 3rd Edition*. New York: McGraw-Hill/Irwin.

Covey, S. R. 1989. *The Seven Habits of Highly Effective People: Restoring the Character Ethic*. New York: Simon and Schuster.

Dye, C. 2000. *Executive Excellence: Protocols for Healthcare Leaders, 2nd Edition*. Chicago: Health Administration Press.

————. 2000. *Leadership in Healthcare: Values at the Top*. Chicago: Health Administration Press.

Dunn, R. T. 2002. *Haimann's Healthcare Management, 7th Edition*. Chicago: Health Administration Press.

Evashwick, C. (editor). 2005. *The Continuum of Long-Term Care, 3rd Edition*. Albany, NY: Delmar Publishers.

Evashwick, C., and T. Holt. 2000. *Integrated Long-Term Care, Acute Care, and Housing.* St. Louis, MO: Catholic Health Association of the United States.

Fried, B. J., and J. A. Johnson (editors). 2002. *Human Resources in Healthcare: Managing for Success.* Chicago: Health Administration Press.

Gift, R. G., and C. F. Kinney (editors). 1996. *Today's Management Methods: A Guide for the Health Care Executive.* Chicago: American Hospital Publishing.

Ginter, P. M., L. E. Swayne, and W. J. Duncan. 2002. *Strategic Management of Health Care Organizations, 4th Edition.* Oxford, UK: Blackwell Publishers.

Griffith, J. R., V. K. Sahney, and R. A. Mohr. 1995. *Reengineering Health Care: Building on CQI.* Chicago: Health Administration Press.

Griffith, J. R. 1996. *The Moral Challenges of Health Care Management.* Chicago: Health Administration Press.

Griffith, J. R., and K. R. White. 2002. *The Well-Managed Healthcare Organization, 5th Edition.* Chicago: Health Administration Press.

Health Administration Press. 2001. *Back to Basics: Foundations of Healthcare Management.* Chicago: Health Administration Press.

Hertzberg, F. 1996. *Work and the Nature of Man.* Cleveland, OH: World Publishing.

Hertzberg, F., B. Mausner, and B. Snyderman. 1967. *The Motivation to Work, 2nd Edition.* New York: John Wiley and Sons.

Hofmann, P. B., and W. A. Nelson (editors). 2001. *Managing Ethically: An Executive's Guide.* Chicago: Health Administration Press.

Kouzes, J. M., and B. Z. Posner. 2002. *The Leadership Challenge, 3rd Edition*. San Francisco: Jossey Bass.

Kovner, A. R., and D. Neuhauser (editors). 2001. *Health Services Management: Readings and Commentary, 7th Edition*. Chicago: Health Administration Press.

Kruger-Wilson, C., and T. Porter-O'Grady. 1999. *Leading the Revolution in Healthcare, 2nd Edition*. Gaithersburg, MD: Aspen Publishers.

Maslow, A. 1943. "A Theory of Human Motivation." *Psychological Review* 50 (7): 370–96.

McGregor, D. 1960. *The Human Side of Enterprise*. New York: McGraw Hill.

———. 1985. *The Human Side of Enterprise, 2nd Edition*. New York: McGraw-Hill.

O'Malley, J. F. 2001. *Healthcare Marketing, Sales, and Service*. Chicago: Health Administration Press.

Pratt, J. 2000. *Long Term Care: Managing Across the Continuum*. Gaithersburg, MD: Aspen Publishers.

Ross, A., F. J. Wenzel, and J. W. Mitlyng. 2002. *Leadership for the Future: Core Competencies in Healthcare*. Chicago: Health Administration Press.

Rynne, T. J. 1995. *Healthcare Marketing in Transition*. New York: McGraw-Hill.

Sturm, A. 1998. *New Rules of Healthcare Marketing*. Chicago: Health Administration Press.

Taylor, F. 1911. *Shop Management*. New York: Harper and Brothers.

Index

Health Insurance Portability and Accountability Act (HIPAA), 24, 159-160, 185

Health promotion, 19

Health status information, 155

Hierarchy of needs theory, 8, 9

Home assessment, 177

Home care, 19, 20

Hospice, 20

Housing services, 19

Human resources (HR): challenges, 45; compensation issues, 45-47; compensation plans, 53-54; competencies, 44-45; director, 47; employee motivation, 57-58; employment advertisements, 48-49; functions, 47-63; hiring process, 49-53; interview process, 52-53; labor relations, 59-61; management team issues, 81; performance appraisal, 54-57; plan, 63, 66-68; recruitment, 48-49; regulation compliance, 61-63; training, 58-59; turnover rates, 46-47

Hygiene factors, 8-9, 10

Impairment, 33

Improvement programs, 146-147

Indemnity insurance, 92-93

Informal support information, 156

Information: sets, 152; sharing, 23-24; technology, 161-162

Inputs, 10

Instrumental activities of daily living (IADL), 31-32

Insurance, 92-93, 97

Integrated financing, 24

Integrated information system (IIS): client information, 155-157; definition, 152; information sharing, 23-24; management's role, 160-162; model, 153-159; privacy, 159-160; security, 159

Integration mechanisms, 21-24

Integrity, 204

Inter-entity management coordination, 22

Internal resources, 114, 116

Interpersonal competencies, 200-201

Intervention, 146

Interviews, 52-53

Job description: information gathering for, 49, 52 ; purpose of, 49; staff psychologist, 50-51

Joint Commission on Accreditation of Healthcare Organizations (JCAHO), 141

Key job identification, 66

Labor: costs, 97; market analysis, 63; relations, 59-61, 67-68

Language issues, 36

Leadership: competencies, 199-201; definition of, 3; development, 7; executive style, 205-206; management versus, 3-4; relationship skills, 201-205; styles, 10-11; ten commitments of, 5; traits, 4-6

Legislation, 24-26

License: authorities, 139; criteria, 138, 140; fees, 140

Life Safety Code, 172-173

Loans, 101

Lobbying activities, 26

Managed care, 93

Management: attitude, 8; competencies, 12-13; definition of, 3; ethical behavior assessment, 191; ethics, 187-190; evaluation tools, 11; focus, 3; integrated information system, 160-162; leadership versus, 3-4; styles, 10-11; theories, 6-10; training, 58

Management team: authorities, 79-80; benefits, 73-74; composition, 75-76; development, 74-75, 76-79; drawbacks, 74-75; functions, 80-82; size, 75-76; structure, 79-80; types of, 72-73

Managerial grid theory, 10

Manpower plan, 63

Marketing: clients, 128-129; four Ps, 124-127; four Rs, 127-128; plan, 130-131; promotional initiative, 132-133; staff involvement in, 131-132; strategic plan relationship, 129-131

Market segmentation, 130-131

Maslow's hierarchy of needs, 8, 9

Meals on Wheels, 20

Medicaid: certification, 141; drawbacks, 90; overview, 88, 90; patients' rights, 37; quality assurance committee, 144; services, 89, 91

Medicare: certification, 141-142; minimum data set, 94; overview, 88; patients' rights, 37; prospective payment system, 95; quality assurance committee, 144; services, 89

Medicare+Choice, 93

Medicare Prescription Drug Improvement and Modernization Act, 88

Medi-Medi, 90

Mentally retarded, 35

Mentoring skills, 203-204

Minimum data set (MDS), 93

Mission statement, 108, 110

Motivating factors, 8-9, 10

Motivation, 4, 57-58

Myers-Briggs instrument, 11

Name policy, 35

National Advisory Board for Nursing Home Examiners (NAB), 12-13

Niche strategy, 130

Objectives, 118, 119

Occupational Safety and Health Act, (OSHA), 173

Older Americans Act (OAA), 90, 131

On-site survey, 142

On-the-job training, 58

Operations review, 80-81

Organizational structure, 77

Orientation, 58

Outputs, 10

Outreach, 19, 133

Participant, 33, 35

Participation competencies, 200

Partnering skills, 202

Patient: confidentiality, 184-185; terminology, 33

Patient's Self Determination Act (PSDA), 181

Patients' rights, 37

Payment information, 159

Payment systems, 94-96

Performance appraisal, 54-57

Personal care assistant, 46

Personal contacts, 132-133

Personal health information, 160

Persons with disabilities, 34-35

Physical environment, 166-168

Physical plant resources, 116

Pregnancy Discrimination Act, 62

Privacy, 159-160

Privacy Rule, 160

Private funding source, 92-94

Probationary period, 57

Program of All-Inclusive Care for the Elderly (PACE), 93

Progressive discipline, 55-57

Promotional initiative, 132-133

Provider: client relationships, 29-30; cultural sensitivity, 36; integration across multiple, 159; name policy, 35

Public relations, 133

Quality assurance program, 145

Quality of healthcare, 143

Quality management, 146-147

Quality measures, 137-138

Recruitment, 48-49, 127-128

Referral patterns, 114

Referrals, 128

Regulation review, 81-82

Rehabilitation facility, 20

Reimbursement, 67, 94

About the Authors

Dr. Connie Evashwick, Sc.D., FACHE

Dr. Evashwick is a Fellow of the American College of Healthcare Executives and an immediate past Regent for District 7. She holds bachelor's and master's degrees from Stanford University and master's and doctoral degrees from the Harvard School of Public Health. Dr. Evashwick is recognized nationally for her expertise in the continuum of care and long-term care delivery systems. Dr. Evashwick's multifaceted career has included positions in direct operations management, consulting, and academia. She has been vice president of long-term care for two major healthcare systems and has consulted with health systems, hospitals, and long-term care organizations across the nation. Dr. Evashwick has authored over 90 publications, including 10 books. Her most recent position has been as the Archstone Foundation Endowed Chair and professor of healthcare administration.

James Riedel, M.B.A., CHE

James Riedel is a certified healthcare executive (CHE) with the American College of Healthcare Executives. He holds a bachelor's degree in marketing from St. Joseph's College in Rensselear, Indiana, and an MBA from Roosevelt University in Chicago. Mr. Riedel's career in hospital administration has spanned 34 years and he has been vice president for four major healthcare facilities in California and the Midwest. During this time, he has taught for 16 years in the graduate school of healthcare administration at California State University–Long Beach as adjunct faculty. Recently retired from his hospital career, Mr. Riedel is still part of the faculty at CSULB were he teaches on a part-time basis. He also enjoys pursuing his hobbies of horseback riding and amateur (ham) radio. He lives with his wife in San Clemente, California.

.